THE WH
CAR OWNER'S

THE WHICH? CAR OWNER'S MANUAL

Peter Burgess

WHICH? BOOKS

CONSUMERS' ASSOCIATION

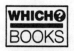

Which? Books are commissioned and researched by
The Association for Consumer Research
and published by Consumers' Association,
2 Marylebone Road, NW1 4DF

Distributed by The Penguin Group:
Penguin Books Ltd, 27 Wrights Lane, London W8 5TZ

Chapter 13, 'Your legal rights', by Keith Richards,
barrister for Consumers' Association

First edition September 1994

British Library Cataloguing in Publication Data
Burgess, Peter
Which? Car Owner's Manual
I. Title
381.45629222

ISBN 0 85202 526 2

Cover design by Steve Ridgeway
Typographic design by Paul Saunders

Typeset by Litho Link Limited, Welshpool, Powys, Wales

Printed and bound by Firmin-Didot (France)
Groupe Herissey
N° d'impression: 24790

CONTENTS

INTRODUCTION

Perhaps the question motoring writers are asked most frequently is 'What car should I get next?' To save a lot of time and anguished discussion, the most suitable response is 'What car do you want to buy?' Nine times out of ten will come the firm response 'An Astra/Fiesta/Rover 800' . . . or any one of the other 200 different models available new in the UK today. Very, very few people treat car buying with a completely open mind – they know what they want and are looking for confirmation that they have made the right decision. Quite how rationally they made that decision in the first place is often in doubt – most people choose their car in the same way they buy new clothes. A new car has to *feel* right, look good and say a little about its owner.

So, except for a minority of people, the car is something rather special, certainly not another domestic product like a washing machine or television. In some ways that attitude is a good one for all of us, for it means that a huge choice of cars remains available with something to suit (almost) everyone. If car buyers all homed in on the *Which?* Best Buys, the choice might rapidly fall to a quarter of its current level. But, of course, with so much emotion tied up in car ownership, there are plenty of pitfalls for the unwary. This book is here to help guide you through the routine of buying and running a car so that it does not cost you any more money or heartache than it should.

In the next couple of hundred pages is the sort of information that will help to steer you in the right direction while acknowledging that you may not have made the best choice in the first place. So if you have a car which requires a lot of servicing, the book tells you how to make sure those garage costs are kept as low as possible, but at the same time pointing out the pitfalls of moving away from the franchised dealer network. You may have bought a car with an absurdly high insurance rating – there is not much you can do about that in the short term, so the *Manual* tells you how to minimise your bill for insurance cover. When it comes to getting rid of that car you bought for a bargain price two years ago you might well find that no one really wants to know. But there are ways which almost guarantee a sale – these are covered in Chapter 3.

Naturally, there is extensive information on the ins and outs of car purchase. Buying a car, whether new or second-hand, is often an awe-inspiring proposition. While many car dealers have successfully cleaned up their act, the motor trade remains an area treated with suspicion by a large number of buyers. Nowadays, too, we all feel the pressure on us to *negotiate* when buying a car. Some of us are natural born bargainers, many are not. Thankfully, the situation on new car buying is changing quickly, and with many dealers' profit margins cut back, there really is little room for the dealer to manoeuvre. Therefore, the need to negotiate down the price of a new car is falling away, making it easier for everyone to get a car at the best possible price. You still, however, need to make sure you get the best price for your old car – you will find plenty of advice here.

Choosing the right new car, if you are truly open-minded, is a complicated process. The initial cost, the length of the warranty and how much it is likely to depreciate are all important factors. Surveys in *Which?* have repeatedly shown that car owners place a very high priority on reliability and safety. Whether that is always carried through to the choice of car is a moot point, but *Which?* has the best information around on these important factors, and this is drawn on within the book. Of course, the situation is continually changing as car manufacturers improve their products. The reliability of the average car improves a little year by year, but the overall picture – certain makes proving more reliable than others – remains remarkably constant.

Car safety is a different story. In just a couple of years big strides have been made, and it is now common to find safety features on small superminis which were, until recently, the domain of large Volvos. The recent addition of airbags, seat-belt pre-tensioners, stiffer body structures and lots of attention to design detail mean that if you want the best safety features you really have little choice but to buy a brand-new car. But not only does it have to be brand new, it has to have been designed (or redesigned) recently to take advantage of the current safety thinking. So it is important to look carefully at any car you buy, new or second-hand, if you are concerned about safety – we give you the low-down here.

All your legal rights concerned with buying and owning a car are covered in detail in the final chapter of this book. After introducing the different areas of law and how they affect the consumer, it takes you through the five major statutes that protect you, such as the Sale of Goods Act 1979 and the Supply of Goods and Services Act 1982. All aspects of buying a car are explored, including contracts, the particular problems associated with second-hand cars such as 'clocking', the price and the pluses and pitfalls of using credit, delivery, dangerous vehicles and product liability. Car owners' rights, including those connected with repair and servicing, are covered here in depth. Finally, what do you do if you want to complain, and how far can you take it? It is all explained here, whether the complaint can be settled quickly with the trader, or whether you need to involve an ombudsman or trade association, or even take the matter to court.

The Which? Car Owner's Manual applies equally to those owning a brand-new Mercedes-Benz or a second-hand Mini. In addition to the areas outlined above, the book deals with company cars, parking problems and travelling abroad.

CHAPTER 1

BUYING A CAR

Much as we might like to think we act in a totally rational manner, the purchase of a car is, for most people, rarely lacking in emotion. Why else, for example, would a family choose not to buy the car which suited their needs perfectly, on the grounds that their neighbour had recently taken delivery of the same model? Why buy a saloon rather than a more versatile hatchback? For many people the reason is that they still see a saloon as a somewhat classier act which does not have the utilitarian connotations of the hatchback. And are German cars really better engineered than others, Italian cars sportier and Japanese cars more reliable? Historically, this may have been the case, but things change, including cars.

If you are one of the few people who can honestly admit to having no preconceptions about your next car, you need to decide on two things: the size of car you require and how much you can afford to spend. *Which?*, and most motoring publications, have traditionally broken down the field into a number of classifications which scoop up over 90 per cent of the run-of-the-mill cars.

SUPERMINIS

For example: **Ford Fiesta, Nissan Micra, Rover Metro**

These small hatchbacks are very popular as second cars, shopping cars and town cars. Prices start at around £6,000 new.

Many models are sought-after second-hand, putting a premium on their used prices. The smaller-engined, 1.1/1.2 litre models are cheap to run and insure. Some diesels are available, though by no means a universal option. Most cars offer the choice of two or four passenger doors.

MICRO CARS

For example: **Daihatsu Mira, Rover Mini, Subaru Vivio**

These are smaller than a supermini, and the idea is that they are even easier to park and use around town. But most are hardly any cheaper to buy new, and even if your budget is really tight, a used version of one of the recommended superminis makes much more sense.

SMALL FAMILY CARS

For example: **Ford Escort, Rover 200, Vauxhall Astra**

Cars in this class are usually available in a choice of body styles, with hatchbacks most popular, followed by saloons then estates. The best provide comfort for four, though legroom is never going to be as generous as with a full-sized family car. Small family cars are therefore suited to those with young families or couples who need the occasional use of the rear seats for adults.

LARGE FAMILY CARS

For example: **Ford Mondeo, Nissan Primera, Vauxhall Cavalier**

Large family cars should be able to carry five adults and their luggage without a squeeze. There is a wide range, from all the major manufacturers, in saloon, hatchback and estate form. Many models are available as a diesel and/or turbo diesel, as well as with a choice of several petrol engines. This is the most popular size of car to be bought by businesses for their fleets so there are plenty around second-hand, often having covered higher-than-average mileages.

EXECUTIVE CARS

For example: **BMW 5 Series, Ford Granada, Rover 800**

These large, costly cars should carry five adults and their luggage in comfort and provide brisk acceleration and relaxed cruising. Most achieve this aim, as well as offering lots of equipment as standard. The chief bugbears are the high running costs and, on most models, alarmingly high depreciation, which makes a nearly new executive car a good buy. Saloons are the popular choice, though estates are common and hatchbacks available from some manufacturers.

OFF-ROADERS

For example: **Land Rover Discovery, Mitsubishi Shogun**

Large four-wheel-drive vehicles have become increasingly popular in recent years, despite fewer than 10 per cent ever being used in the sticky, off-road conditions for which they were designed. Sitting high up in a large vehicle seems to give drivers a sense of security. Against this, comfort levels, performance, running costs and, surprisingly, space, can be inferior to those of a decent large estate car. Turbo-diesels offer passable economy – perhaps 25 mpg – compared with under 20 mpg for most petrol-engined off-roaders.

MULTI-PURPOSE VEHICLES

For example: **Mitsubishi Space Wagon, Renault Espace, Toyota Previa**

These tall, spacious vehicles offer the virtues of a traditional estate car but with the benefit of a third row of seats, giving room for seven or eight. Being purpose-designed, they generally offer more in the way of comfort than an estate car with an optional third seat in the boot, but there is rarely room for a full complement of passengers and a load of luggage at the same time. The most popular models are the Mitsubishi Space Wagon, Nissan Serena, Renault Espace and Toyota Previa and older Space Cruiser.

WHAT TO LOOK OUT FOR IN A NEW CAR

What are the key criteria on which you should base your choice of new car? Once you have decided upon the size and style of vehicle, two factors have traditionally come out as highly important for *Which?* members: **safety** (covered in detail in Chapter 8) and **reliability**.

Reliability

Reliability is a characteristic which depends not only on the make and model of car, but also its age and the use to which it has been put. The picture is constantly changing, as some manufacturers strive to improve upon a poor record, and others become complacent. *Which?* reports on reliability in its annual *Guide to New and Used Cars* published each June. Makes which have consistently stood out as having above-average reliability are Honda, Mazda, Mercedes-Benz, Mitsubishi, Nissan and Toyota; relative newcomer Proton looks good too.

Value for money

Other factors will have a strong influence on your choice. Value for money must be a strong concern, and it is in this pursuit that you are likely to run across two common motor-industry marketing ploys. The first is the **special edition**. This model will be heavily promoted in the press, both national and regional, as well as in the dealer showroom. It will usually combine some eye-catching stickers on the bodywork (or 'graphics', as the trade likes to call them), a special and equally eye-catching cloth trim on the seats, a few tempting 'extras' – a sunroof is the favourite – and the promise that this car is just one of 500, 1,000, 2,000 (take your pick) of a limited edition.

Attractive pricing is also a feature of the special edition, but here a certain level of caution is needed. First, often (but not always), the special is built by taking the rock-bottom model in the range and making eye-catching but ultimately low-cost changes to give it some life. You are likely, therefore, to find that under all the glitz, you are left with a pretty basic car. Second, discounts are generally much tougher to negotiate on a special edition, so in reality there may be less difference than you thought between the price of the special and that of a better model where a good discount is readily available. Third, when you come to sell a special edition in years to come, you will find that the motor trade tends to judge its used value on that basic model, which may mean it is worth less than you hoped.

The second ploy to be wary of is the **run-out model**, a situation which occurs around the time of a model change. The car manufacturer and its dealers are quite likely to find that at the time when they want to launch a new model there are still plenty of examples of the old car left 'in the system'. Many potential buyers will know about the new car and will therefore wait for its appearance, realising that there will be numerous improvements in the design. It becomes increasingly difficult to sell the remainder of the old cars, so the manufacturer can either resort to 'special-editioning' it, or to offering the standard car at a cut price.

As long as you get the car at the right price, a run-out model can be fabulous value. What is worrying, though, is that some buyers seem unaware precisely what they are buying, so it is always worth asking a dealer when a particular car is going to be superseded by a new model.

Other considerations

Of course, dozens of other factors may be important to you, some more so than others. Comfort, boot space, colour and the design of the dashboard are just a few of the things which can make a car good – or a complete no-hoper – for you. If you are truly open-minded, then the *Which?* Best Buys and recommendations make the sensible starting point for narrowing your choice. If you already have an idea, then the *Which?* report on the model you fancy needs investigating, if only to put yourself fully in the picture on the pros and cons.

However you select your next car, nothing compares with visiting a showroom, giving the car the once-over and taking a test drive. Only then will you find if there is some terrible quirk in the design which you could not possibly live with – and it is a far better idea to find that out before you have closed the deal.

Where to buy a new car

Franchised dealers – dealers appointed and approved by the car manufacturers – are the only reliable source of new cars in the

UK. Much has been written in the past about the inequalities in car pricing between the UK and the rest of Europe, and it has proved a viable option for some to import a UK specification, right-hand-drive car from the European mainland. There are European Commission rules which are supposed to stop the difference between selling prices in member countries varying too much, although they are not properly enforced. The fluidity in exchange rates and the undoubted complication involved in personally importing a car, however, make buying a car from another European country an option only for the most determined buyer.

Franchised dealers

Car manufacturers and importers are allowed to restrict the sale of their new cars to their authorised dealers. The trade bodies involved have persuaded the European Commission that this is vital because cars are highly complicated items which need specialist attention. The downside for the car buyer is that the element of competition is reduced. You cannot compare prices for the same car within the same town in the way in which you might walk along the high street seeing which shop is selling a pair of jeans at the lowest price, because few towns have more than one dealer selling each make. In any case, the list price would be the same.

On the other hand, no matter where you buy your new car, the warranty and servicing work can be carried out at a dealer of your choice for that make. This gives you the opportunity to shop around the UK to get the best deal, yet have the car looked after by your local franchised dealer just as if you had bought it there. And shopping around is the name of the game when it comes to buying a new car. Salesmen *expect* to be asked for discounts, so the price you pay will depend to an extent upon your willingness to negotiate.

How much discount can you hope for? Until recently a franchised dealer worked generally with a gross profit margin of around 17 per cent. From that the dealer had to meet all his overheads, pay his salesmen's commission and make his profit. Recently this situation has changed, with the dealer margin cut back to the 10 or even 5 per cent mark. On balance that is good news for the car buyer because there is less need to battle hard to get the best price – the scope for huge discounts is no longer there.

Indeed, you will now find it difficult to get discounts on quite a few makes. Certain manufacturers, such as Mercedes-Benz, have rarely needed to barter with customers over price. Others have models which are never in abundant supply – the Mitsubishi Space Wagon, for example. And a new development is for the manufacturer or importer to cut out the dealer margin completely, paying instead a handling charge of a few hundred pounds for each car sold.

Despite these changes, there will always be times when a manufacturer, importer or dealer is desperate to sell cars no matter what, and then some real bargains can be had. It remains a common practice for franchised dealers to be offered occasional incentives to sell more cars, and if you are lucky much of that extra money might come in your direction in the form of an additional discount. There is no clear way of finding out about these promotions (they are certainly not advertised as such to the public and often run for just a month or two) other than talking to several dealers to see if anything comes up.

Dealing with dealers

While it is undoubtedly more convenient to telephone dealers to discuss prices of new cars, the face-to-face approach can be more beneficial in the long run. A salesman will see that you are making a serious enquiry, yet you can let him know that you will be asking other dealers to quote for the same car. That way you should be able to impress upon him or her that you are genuinely interested, yet you will not buy a car at an unrealistic price.

Some times are better than others to talk to dealers. Two or three days before a month's end the salesman will have a good idea whether or not that month's sales targets are likely to be met. If business has not been good, you may find that an extra few hundred pounds' reduction is available, as long as you are prepared to tie up the deal immediately.

Certain times of year are better for a discount. While most new cars are sold in January (so the car is registered in that year rather than in the previous one) or August (for the new registration letter) the preceding months can be very quiet in the car showrooms and consequently a good time to negotiate hard for a better-than-average discount. The reduction does, however, *need* to be better than you would get in January or August because the car you buy will eventually be worth a few hundred pounds less when you come to sell it later. September is a good compromise: your new car will still have the latest registration letter, yet dealers will be keen to sell after the August rush has died down.

On-the-road charges

Some words of warning: the 'list price' of a new car, with the occasional exception, does not include the 'on-the-road' charges. These are made up of a delivery charge, the pre-delivery inspection, number plates, road fund licence, fuel and, possibly, the charge for the first service. Car manufacturers are compelled to quote a fixed price for the cost of delivery, the pre-delivery inspection, plates and service, and you should find them tucked away on the price list. These four elements typically add up to around £400, with a year's road fund licence and fuel adding perhaps another £150.

When you are asking for quotations, make sure that you are quoted the final 'on-the-road' cost. While this makes calculating the precise discount you are getting a little more difficult, you do end up comparing like with like.

Car brokers

Car brokers are an alternative source of new cars – you will find several companies advertising in the back pages of *What Car?* magazine. Brokers obtain brand-new cars through franchised dealers, in the same way that any customer would. But because they buy a lot of cars, they should be getting the best possible discounts, which they pass on to you after taking one or two per cent for their trouble.

To use a broker, simply telephone and get a quotation for the car in which you are interested. The price will almost certainly be an on-the-road figure, and if nothing else, you can use this as a guideline when negotiating face-to-face with a dealer.

If you decide to buy through a broker you need to take particular care about how you do business. You may be asked for a deposit once your order is taken, which is not unreasonable. There is, however, a somewhat greater element of risk buying through a broker than dealing directly with a franchised dealer – some brokers have nothing more than a telephone, a desk and a list of contacts. That is not to say that they do not do a good job, just that, from the customer's point of view, the security of dealing with a large reputable company is not necessarily there.

You should, therefore, make sure your deposit is either a nominal one – £100 at the most – or that it goes direct to the dealer. For the latter to happen, it is vital that you know who the dealer is and make your cheque out to that company – feel free to telephone the dealer directly to check that everything is OK. When it comes to taking delivery of the car, it is absolutely *vital* that the balance is paid to the dealer. If you pay the broker who, for whatever reason, does not settle up with the dealer, the legal title to the car does not transfer to you. The dealer will be within his rights to take that car back and you will be left trying to recover the sum from the broker.

If all this sounds too terrifying, rest assured that plenty of people have bought new cars through brokers. The best advice is to seek out one who never takes any money from the client but is paid his or her commission by the dealer.

NEARLY NEW CARS

If you cannot afford the new car you really hanker after, an almost-new one might be the answer. Cars depreciate most heavily in their first year, so even on the smallest car you can expect to make savings of £1,000 if you buy an example between three and twelve months old.

Everyone in the motor trade is keen on being seen as successful, and for the manufacturers and importers that means 'selling' many new cars. In reality, however, it is registrations, not the actual sales that are recorded, and there are a few well-known dodges which increase the new car registration figures without the cars actually being sold to a customer. Eventually, these cars have to find their way to a genuine buyer, which is why there is often a good supply of pre-registered, but almost-new, cars on the market.

These 'nearly new' cars originate from three main sources. The first is a dealer's own stock of demonstration vehicles, which have been registered and run for a few months before selling. The mileage is generally low – perhaps a few thousand miles recorded – though some cars get used more heavily by staff as personal transport during the evenings and at weekends, so may have covered up to 10,000 miles.

The second route for nearly new models to the dealers' forecourts is through the manufacturers' own fleets. Company cars abound at the locations of the car manufacturers and their importers, and the stock of cars tends to be turned over very frequently. These are then sold directly to the franchised dealers.

The third major source, and the oddest, is through the rental market. A few of the major manufacturers encourage the big car rental companies to replace their cars every few months by offering huge discounts. They are often hired out on the Channel Islands, where speed limits are low and distances short, so that by the time they are ready to be replaced, they have often covered just two or three thousand miles. They are then sold through auction and, often, purchased by major franchised dealers for sale to the public.

You should have no major worries about buying a car like this. The warranty will still be in force, the car will almost certainly have been serviced correctly and the condition should be little different from a brand-new model. But before you sign on the dotted line, check that the price you are paying is a good bit less than the *discount* price of a brand-new example.

WHERE TO BUY A USED CAR

There are three basic sources of used cars: dealers, private advertisers and auctions. Each has its advantages and disadvantages, and you will find buyers who swear by each method. Before you make up your mind, weigh up carefully the pros and cons below.

Dealers

For:

- You will find a large choice of cars at one location.
- The dealer may take your car in part exchange. Even if he does not want it for his own forecourt, he will sell it on through his trade sources.
- Used cars should have been prepared for sale, so that faults have been dealt with, and the car is clean and presentable.
- You should have an opportunity to inspect the car carefully, and to take it for a test drive.
- A dealer who has nothing to hide will be happy for you to get the car professionally inspected by the AA and RAC.
- Some form of guarantee will be offered.
- You have much better legal comeback if things do not work out.
- You have better protection if the car you buy turns out to be stolen or on hire purchase.
- Dealers may be able to find a hard-to-locate car for you.

Against:

- Buying from a dealer invariably means buying at higher prices, as the company has its profit margin to add to the cost of the deal. Even so, 'trade dealers' may offer cars at prices you find difficult to match privately.
- You are not going to find out much about the previous history of the car.

Private sales

For:

- The cost of a car bought privately should be lower than that from a dealer.
- You should be able to question the previous owner about the history of the car (particularly on whether it has been involved in any accidents), the servicing and reliability.

Against:
- The facilities offered to you for inspecting the car might be minimal.
- There could be insurance worries when you take a test drive. Unless the seller has comprehensive insurance for 'any driver' you will have to rely on your own insurance. That means you will be covered only if you are a policy holder (and not a 'spouse' or a 'named driver') and only for third party cover. That could result in difficulties as to who will pay for damage to the car should you be involved in an accident.
- Your legal rights if the car turns out to be faulty are very much more limited than if you bought from a dealer (see Chapter 13). At most the car 'should correspond with the description', so keep a copy of the advert, and take someone along as a witness to what is said when you negotiate the deal.

Auctions

For:
- Prices are almost certainly the lowest around.
- There will be a wide choice of cars.
- The deal is tied up very quickly.

Against:
- Usually there's the opportunity for only a superficial inspection of the car.
- There's no chance of a test drive.
- Your legal rights are minimal if you buy a lemon (see Chapter 13).
- Bidding at auction is an acquired art.

USED-CAR ADS, AND HOW TO READ THEM

An advertisement for a second-hand car should give sufficient information for you to judge whether your time will be well spent following up the matter. The key ingredients to look for, and to discuss on the telephone if they are missing from the advertisement, are:

- the year the car was first registered
- the registration letter – for example, 1989 'G'
- the size of engine
- the trim level – for example, 'GL', 'Merit'
- the mileage, to the nearest 1,000
- how much MOT is left to run – for cars over 3 years old
- the price
- the location – you will need to decide how far you are prepared to travel.

Surprisingly, these vital details are often incomplete in used-car advertisements. Dealer ads, particularly, omit unflattering details, though most dealers will ensure a car has a full MOT even if they do not mention it in writing.

What about the condition of the car? Treat any mention of a car's condition, either verbally or in an advertisement, with great caution – you should always try to discover for yourself if what is claimed about a car is really true. Keep a copy of what was written in the advertisement, as it gives you solid grounds for redress should the car not live up to its promise. Chapter 2 covers checking over a used car yourself.

Advertisement jargon buster

Car ads are full of abbreviations – these are some of the most common:

A/C air-conditioning

ABS anti-lock brakes

C/L central locking

E/W electric windows

ESR electric sunroof

EDM electric door mirrors

EHDM electric heated door mirrors

FSH full service history

4WD four-wheel drive

HRW heated rear window

LWB long wheelbase

LHD left-hand drive

LSD limited slip differential

PAS power-assisted steering

RHR rear head restraints

SWB short wheelbase

WHAT IS THAT SECOND-HAND CAR REALLY WORTH?

Your initial feeling about the value of a car has to be based on what price the seller is asking. Whether it appears in an advert in a newspaper or on a windscreen sticker on the dealer's forecourt, it is a starting point for working out the true value.

But you need to be careful. It is highly risky to take an advertised price of a single car and use it as the only basis for negotiation. Remember that if you were the seller, you might well decide to ask £1,000 more than the car is worth in the hope of finding just one unsuspecting buyer. So look around at what is on offer in your area, either in your local paper or in a regional car advertiser like *Auto Trader,* to get a better feel of the true market values. That is as good a way as any of making sure that you are not starting off on the wrong foot when the real negotiations begin.

Used-car price guides

The motor trade relies on two guides to used-car prices: *Glass's* and *CAP*. Both are admirably clear and comprehensive, but rely on the dealer using his own experience to adjust the published values according to the particular circumstances of the day. To avoid any risk of argument between the public and dealers, these two guides can only be purchased by genuine motor traders.

An alternative to the trade guides is to buy one of the several monthly bookstall publications, which list, in incredible detail, values of used cars. There can, however, be wild differences between these figures and those in *Glass's* and *CAP*, which means that a used-car salesman will take a deep breath as he tries to explain why your calculations do not match up with his. However, such guides are a reasonable starting point, particularly in a private purchase.

Retail, trade and private values

Used-car price guides usually give several values for the same car, with 'retail' or 'first class' at one end of the scale, and 'trade' at the other. The 'retail value' is the sticker price you will see on a garage forecourt. It is the maximum possible amount you should pay for a car and this cost should include a warranty of some sort, a full valet, the opportunity to arrange finance, and the offer of part exchange on your old car. The price also includes the dealer's profit margin, which is, of course, a solid reason for the price to be at its highest.

The 'trade value', at the other end of the spectrum, is the lowest value of the car and the starting point for a car taken in part exchange. This is the price a dealer might pay for your car if he were buying it for cash, so that he could then tidy it up and sell it at retail price. It is also the price which will be more or less reflected at the car auctions. Trade price is not necessarily the same as a dealer will allow you when you want to part exchange your old car. Quite often you can expect to better 'trade' when you part exchange, though much will depend upon on how easily and quickly the dealer thinks he can sell your old car.

So what about the private sale? Many sellers fall into the trap of seeing a price for a car like theirs on a garage forecourt and thinking they deserve the same when they sell it privately. The private buyer has to watch out for this, because it makes no sense at all to pay forecourt prices to a private seller who can offer none of the advantages of a dealer. The true value of a car in a private sale should fall somewhere between the trade and retail prices, so the seller makes more than trade, and the buyer makes a useful saving on dealing with a garage.

Used values and the car's history

Even if you think you have calculated a fair price for a second-hand car, there are factors about any car which can alter that value significantly.

Condition

If it is less than perfect you should subtract anything between 10 and 30 per cent.

Mileage

The mileage has a huge effect on the value of a second-hand car which is why clocking – illegally winding back the mileage recorder – is such a major problem in the used-car trade. The 'average' car covers perhaps 10,000 to 12,000 miles per annum in its first three years, then 8,000 to 10,000 miles per annum after that. But with over half of new cars reckoned to be bought by businesses, plenty of used cars have covered 50,000 to 60,000 miles in the first three years of their life.

It is impossible to give an adjustment factor which will apply to all cars, as the effect of high mileage on used prices differs according to the model and its age. But as an example, the value of a 3-year-old car which has covered 60,000 miles instead of 30,000 miles would be reduced by:

- supermini, like a Fiesta £750
- small family cars, like the Escort £1,200
- large family cars, like the Sierra £1,400
- executive cars, like the Granada £1,800.

Do not place too much emphasis on low mileage. Excessively low mileage often means lots of short trips to the shops. With little chance for the engine to get thoroughly warm on each journey, wear can be *worse* than on a car which has covered a much higher mileage on motorways. Also, there is always the fear of clocking – see Chapter 2.

Registration letter

Cars registered after 1 August get the latest registration letter, and this has a strong effect on the second-hand value in years to come. Once again it is impractical to give precise figures, as these vary with the model and age of car, but, for example, the additional second-hand value of a 1991 car with a 'J' instead of an 'H' plate is roughly:

- supermini, like a Fiesta £400
- small family cars, like the Escort £600
- large family cars, like the Sierra £650
- executive cars, like the Granada £800.

These differences reduce as the cars get older.

Extras

Sellers are generally very keen to point out the optional extras fitted to their car and how they increase the value. By all means let this sway you into buying one car in preference to another, but do not pay any more than you would for the standard car, unless it is almost new. On the used market extras lose virtually all of their value very quickly, so when you later come to part exchange this car you are unlikely to find a dealer who will make you much of an allowance for them.

DEPRECIATION – AVOIDING THE WORST EXCESSES

Buyers of both new and used cars ignore the spectre of depreciation at their peril. While it is easy enough to name a dozen different new cars costing within pounds of each other, you can rest assured that the long-term picture will vary dramatically, with the best of the bunch losing perhaps £2,000 in value over the first year, compared with £4,000 for the worst.

It is important to make sure that the new car you buy is not only affordable, but that you will get a reasonable sum when you come to sell or part exchange it. On the other hand, the used-car buyer can get something rather special at a bargain price – an Alfa instead of an Astra, for instance – as long as he or she is prepared to live with certain characteristics of the Alfa which undoubtedly put off a lot of used-car buyers. The key criteria which force down second-hand values are a combination of the following:

Expensive servicing Dealers may charge high rates, spares might be pricey, or the car may be 'old' technology or very complicated, which tends to push up the bills.

Poor record for corrosion This always frightens people off, even if the big problems occurred 10 years ago – still a stigma with Italian cars.

Poor reliability Unreliability and bad build quality go hand-in-hand. The cost of fixing an unreliable car may not be high, but the irritation factor is.

Image Dull, plain and boring cars are acceptable at the bottom end of the market as long as they have other virtues. The old Nissan Micra, for example, was all these but reliable and very easy to drive and so popular second-hand. But at the other end of the scale, an indifferent image in an executive car – like that of the Nissan Maxima – means depreciation is heavy.

Heavy discounting If a manufacturer supports heavy discounts to its dealers, used values will be correspondingly lower. There are many reasons why a BMW 3 Series is worth 88 per cent of its original list price after one year, while a Cavalier fetches only 63 per cent, but the easy availability of a hefty discount on the Cavalier in the first place is a major factor.

Hefty insurance This has seriously hit the values of used GTis and other high-performance cars.

Colour Cars in 'boring' colours (dark blue, beige, brown) are just not sought after by most buyers, who seem to prefer red, white, black or a metallic paint finish. A car in a dull colour can be worth hundreds of pounds less than an identical model in a bright finish.

WARRANTIES – WATCH OUT!

First, let's clear up any confusion about warranties and guarantees. They are the same thing, and if someone says they are not, you have every right to suspect that they are trying to pull the wool over your eyes.

New car warranties

New cars come with two or three types of warranty. The first is a general catch-all, covering the mechanical components, paint, trim and interior – pretty much the whole car. This usually lasts for just 12 months, though an increasing number of manufacturers are offering 24- or 36-month guarantees. In addition, there will almost certainly be a 'corrosion' warranty, which covers serious rust but not deterioration of the paintwork. Finally, a few manufacturers make a point of offering a specific guarantee to cover the paint. (See Appendix 6 for a list of new car guarantees.)

The standard warranty

This is the part that everyone relies on with a new car to sort out teething troubles during the first year(s) of ownership. It will also cover the more serious eventualities like a blown engine or faulty transmission. Strictly speaking the dealer is obliged only to fix the fault, not necessarily fit a brand new part or offer you a loan car while yours is in dock.

Quite how strongly the dealer adheres to the letter of the written warranty will depend largely on the back-up he gets from the manufacturer. Some dealers will not budge an inch, others, notably at the more prestige end of the market, adopt a more flexible approach. Do not get grand ideas about the dealer replacing your car with another, or giving you your money back, if your new car turns out to be more trouble than you are prepared to accept. You could try, but the number of customers who have successfully been down this avenue is tiny.

Extending your new-car warranty by a year or two is worth considering, though the price can be high and often the cover is reduced over that in the original guarantee. You could also find that to keep the warranty valid it is compulsory to have the car serviced at a main dealer. No matter how new your car, any guarantee will almost certainly exclude the cost of parts which wear, like the clutch, brake linings and tyres.

Corrosion warranty

By and large this part of the warranty covers only rust working its way through from the inside of the car to the outside. Beware: some cars require a compulsory check every year or two, and if you miss it your warranty may be invalidated. Surface rust is not usually covered – you are meant to spot this yourself and get it attended to at your own cost.

Paintwork warranty

This covers most of the parts left out of the corrosion warranty. But it still excludes surface rust caused by damage, typically from stone chips and car park knocks. You should touch these in yourself as soon as possible.

Goodwill payments

There is still hope if you have problems after the warranty has lapsed. You will have to pay for any repairs to be carried out (preferably by a franchised dealer for your make), but then ask him to put in for a 'goodwill' payment. As long as your service record is complete, preferably with an authorised dealer, you may find the manufacturer will give a sympathetic refund of part of the cost.

Used-car warranties

It is easy to get what is often referred to as a 'warranty' on a second-hand car. Any dealer will supply one or, if you have bought privately, you can take one out yourself. The 'warranty' on a second-hand car pushes up its price, however, so if you decide that you do not want one, you are entirely justified in asking the dealer to reduce the cost of the car.

But the major point about these so-called warranties is that in reality they are mostly insurance policies and thus not like the new-car warranty at all. The motor industry's Code of Practice says they should be described as Mechanical Breakdown Insurance (MBI), though as this does not sound as attractive to potential buyers, many dealers still use the incorrect term. Consequently, what happens when you make a claim is rather different to the situation with a new-car warranty. If something goes wrong, the garage carrying out the repair puts in a claim to the insurance company and, assuming the work is covered, the bill is settled.

What fools many used-car buyers is their expectation of precisely what is covered. These MBIs rarely provide cover as comprehensive as that which you get with a new car, with the poorest excluding everything but the engine, gearbox, axle, steering and suspension, perhaps to a limit of a few hundred pounds *and* with stringent servicing requirements. Others – the more costly examples, especially those backed by the manufacturer – offer much more, but may still exclude the parts, like the clutch, most likely to cause problems.

There is nothing wrong with used-car MBIs, but do not expect them to provide a universal remedy if things go wrong. Look carefully at the policy document and make sure that it gives you the protection you need *before* you accept it. Too many restrictions could mean you would be better placed having the money knocked off the price of the car.

CHAPTER 2

Checking Over a Used Car

Locating an attractive example of the second-hand car you fancy, at the right sort of price, is only half the battle. You then need to take great pains to check that the car you are being offered is what it appears to be, and is as good as the seller maintains. After weeks of searching through the small ads and garage forecourts, it is all too easy to jump feet first into trouble when what looks like the right car finally turns up. The safest attitude you can adopt is always to be prepared to turn heel and walk away unless you are totally convinced the car is exactly what you want.

Ten Key Questions to Ask the Seller

Before you even start looking the car over, you may as well get the paperwork out of the way. A number of key issues should affect your buying decision, either by strengthening your negotiating position on the price, or even putting you off the whole deal completely because the paperwork just does not look right.

1 Do you have the original receipt?
This will help confirm that the seller is in fact the genuine owner of the car. It is important to remember that the Vehicle Registration Document is *not* proof of ownership. This records merely who is the registered keeper of the car, which is not the

same thing at all. In some cases, less than reputable companies will register fleet cars in their employees' names so that when the cars come to be sold, they look like they have been used privately rather than for business. All it then takes is for a third party to wind back the odometer and what was recently a high-mileage company car is suddenly a low-mileage privately owned example.

2 Is the car being bought on hire purchase or subject to any form of finance agreement?

It is possible for the seller to produce a receipt and Vehicle Registration Document, yet still not be the true owner. Cars purchased under hire purchase and some other forms of finance agreement are owned by the finance company until the final payment has been made by the purchaser. Though there are sometimes ways of extricating yourself from the mess of buying a car which the seller illegally sold to you (because he or she had not paid off the debt), it is best to be safe in the first place. You can cover yourself by making a check through HPI – see later in this chapter.

3 Did you buy the car from new? If not, whom did you buy it from?

It is useful to get as much detail about the car's past life as possible, as this helps authenticate its history. The Vehicle Registration Document will tell you how many past owners the car has had – again it is generally better to have few rather than many – and it records the name and address of the previous owner. This is useful because you can take a note of that and then telephone the previous owner to check out anything which worries you, such as the recorded mileage. Of course, there is no real reason to assume that the previous owner will be any more honest than the current one, but he or she will have less to lose by telling you the truth.

Also look at the small print on the Vehicle Registration Document, and compare it with the car being sold. Colour, engine capacity, and engine and chassis numbers are all recorded, and it takes a matter of a minute or two to check that these coincide with the colour and the numbers under the bonnet. If they do not, something is seriously wrong.

4 How long have you owned the car?
Generally, a car which has been owned for several years by the same person is a rather more attractive proposition than one which is being sold within a year of purchase. Though a seller may tell you that his or her circumstances have changed since buying the car a few months ago, you should consider whether the true reason is that the car has turned out to be troublesome.

5 How long does the MOT run for?
All cars over three years old need an MOT certificate of roadworthiness (see Chapter 5). Clearly, the longer the certificate still has to run on a second-hand car the better, with the best option being a car sold with a full 12 months to run. Most reputable garages will ensure the used cars they sell have a full MOT certificate, or put the car through a fresh test (and correct any faults which turn up) if you ask. Buying privately, you really need to ask yourself why a car is being sold with an MOT certificate which has only a few months to run – is it because the owner knows that there could be big bills around the corner to get the car through the test? An MOT costs around £25, so if it comes to the crunch, and if you like a car with a short MOT, insist the owner puts it through a fresh test before you make a deal.

6 How much road tax comes with the car?
A road fund licence costs in the region of £130 annually, so a lengthy, unexpired portion of the licence is worth having. Check what is on the car – some dealers will claim back unexpired road tax as soon as they buy a car, leaving the buyer with the task of re-taxing the car on purchase. And make sure that the tax disc is still in the window when you collect a car you have previously inspected.

7 Do you have any 'service history'?
Old MOT certificates, garage bills and a stamped service book are good signs of a car that has been cared for by the owner. If

you are lucky enough to be offered a car where the owner has every MOT certificate since the car was 3 years old, together with servicing receipts from a garage franchised for that make of car, you are as sure as you can be about the genuineness of the vehicle. This past history will also allow you to check that the mileage has been increasing in regular amounts, as this is recorded on both the MOT and the service schedule.

With certain makes of car, mainly at the prestige end of the market, a 'full service history' (or 'fsh' as it is often abbreviated in advertisements) makes a great deal of difference to the second-hand value. Check carefully the documentation if such claims are made, and ensure that the services were carried out at an authorised dealer rather than at just any old garage.

8 Have you had to replace anything recently?

Some parts on a car naturally wear out – tyres, brakes, clutch and exhaust, for example – so a recent replacement of any of these items can generally be considered a good thing. Engines, gearboxes and axles, on the other hand, can last the lifetime of the car if properly cared for, so replacement of these may indicate that the car has had a hard life or that the routine maintenance has been ignored. Any owner who has had one of these major components replaced in the months prior to sale is unlikely to spend the major sums for an authorised replacement unit from a main dealer, and probably has opted for an engine or gearbox from a specialist reconditioner, where standards vary greatly.

9 Has the car ever been involved in an accident?

The car repair and insurance industries would like us to believe that the majority of accident-damaged cars can be repaired so that they are indistinguishable from their pre-accident condition. That may be so, but there still seems to be a great deal of consumer resistance to buying a car which has been involved in a serious accident, for understandable reasons. You should, therefore, pose the question about accidents, though do not necessarily expect a straight answer. Clearly it is particularly difficult for the present owner of a car which has passed through several hands to know the full history, and even if you get the full story there are checks you can make yourself (see later in this chapter).

10 How negotiable are you on the price?
Only the most stubborn seller will dig his or her heels in by sticking to the advertised price. Dealers and private sellers alike expect a bit of bartering to take place, and there is nothing like a potential buyer turning heel to persuade a seller that the price should be dropped a touch more. A seller would be foolish to admit his or her full negotiating position immediately, but there is no harm asking the question to get an idea of the reaction you are going to get after you have looked the car over.

Clocking

Clocking is the winding back of the mileage recorder (strictly speaking, the odometer) to give the impression that a car has had an easier life than it really has. The practice is unfortunately rife, with as many as one in three second-hand cars reckoned to be clocked by dealers or owners. The reason is simple: a low-mileage car is worth hundreds of pounds more than exactly the same model with a high mileage. AA estimates put the value of the total fraud at £100 million every year. It is therefore important to make a few simple checks to ensure that the car you are thinking of buying really has covered just the mileage which appears on the odometer.

The tell-tale signs

Your first action should be to look for signs of excessive wear in the car. The driver's seat should not show much sign of wear if the car has covered only 35,000 miles, so suspect the worst if it does. Look for other signs of deterioration which occur with high mileage, such as worn edges to the pedal rubbers, damaged trim around the door, a key which has become polished smooth through heavy use, and signs of excessive stone chipping on the front edge of the bonnet. Look also for replacements – you should treat a brand-new pedal rubber with the same suspicion as a badly worn one.

Then inspect the odometer itself. It is not always easy to make a perfect job of winding back the 'clock' . Look very closely, and if you see signs of scratching on the face of the numbers, or numbers which do not line up properly, suspect the worst. Look closer still to see if the left-hand digit has been obscured with black paint, an easy way to make a car with 135,000 miles look like it has covered only 35,000.

Study the documentation

Any reputable seller will have the Vehicle Registration Document available – if it is 'with the accountant' or 'delayed in the post/at Swansea', you should tread warily. Note the names of the previous owners from the log book and telephone them to verify the mileage. Some garages make a point of getting a signed declaration from the previous owner as to the mileage, though even this is worth verifying independently. Look too at the service record book and MOT certificates for a steady record of increasing mileages. Make sure nothing is missing or altered in the service record book – and be particularly wary if pages are ripped out.

Buy from a reputable dealer

Your chances of picking up a clocked car are far fewer from an established franchised dealer, especially if the dealer sold the car new. Garages that you have used before and those recommended by friends are less of a risk than those completely new to you. And membership of a trade association, like the Retail Motor Industry Federation or the Scottish Motor Trade Association (see Addresses), though far from an infallible guide to honesty, is better than nothing. Remember, the more reputable the dealer, the more chance you've got of a refund if you car turns out to be clocked.

GETTING PROFESSIONAL HELP

Two valuable types of help are available to the private car buyer, which takes away a lot of the risk involved in the purchase. The first deals with the car's history, the second with a physical inspection of the car.

HPI Autodata

There are certain aspects of a second-hand car which are difficult for the uninitiated to verify. What if the car has been stolen? Has it been involved in a serious accident, then written-off as a lost cause by the insurance company and subsequently rebuilt by a back-street cowboy to look like new? Or is it still owned by the hire purchase or finance company, and not the legal property of the seller at all?

For many years dealers have been able to check out this type of information with the HPI (see page 41 for address). This company has arrangements with insurance and finance companies, and the police, which enables the collection of large amounts of data on car accidents and finance. This information is then sold as a car checking service to the motor trade and, more recently, the general public.

For a fee of around £15, you can get an instant HPI check over the telephone which covers the following areas:

Outstanding finance

This tells you if the seller still owes money on the car. HPI will inform you of the type and date of the finance agreement. Clearly if a car is still subject to an agreement, at the very least the finance company *must* be involved in the sale process. You may feel that you can discuss this point with the seller, or you may decide to abandon the idea of that particular car completely.

Condition alert

This is the list of write-offs, cases where a car was so badly damaged in an accident that the insurer decided to cut its loses and pay the owner the value of the car prior to the accident, rather than getting it repaired. That is not to say it will not get repaired by someone else. The insurer may sell the remains for scrap and the best parts may be salvaged, or the wreck could find its way to a workshop which will rebuild it.

The big worry with this last option is that the insurers had already decided that the cost of repairing the car properly would be more than the final value of the car. So anyone who is going to get the car back on the road has to look at ways of cutting corners to keep the repair costs in check, and you run the risk of buying a sub-standard, even dangerous, car.

Stolen vehicles

If a vehicle has been reported stolen to the police it should show up on this register. Your best bet then is to have nothing more to do with the seller but instead to contact the police – anonymously if you want to. With all these checks a great reliance is placed on the registration number of the car. It is easy enough to put false plates on a car if it is stolen, which is why it is important to look at the paperwork – the registration document and other bits of 'history', like service dockets – to confirm the true identity of the car.

Security watch

Some cars are thought to be of such a high risk of being illegally sold or 'disappearing' that they are automatically registered on the HPI security register. Hire cars and fleet-owned vehicles are the common choices here, so you should be very wary of any car which appears on this list.

The risk factor

What are the chances of the car you are currently considering being on an HPI list? Much will depend upon whom you are buying from. A large, well-established dealership is likely to have made its own checks with HPI, because it would not want to risk compromising its own reputation at a later stage. At the other end of the scale some 'back-street dealers' and private sellers will have no qualms about ripping you off, so these need much more careful attention. HPI's own statistics show that one in three of all private buyers making an enquiry received a warning about the car they were thinking of buying.

How reliable is an HPI check?

As HPI relies on others – the police, finance companies, insurers and so on – to provide the information for its databases total coverage of all the suspect cars on the market is nigh on impossible to achieve. You will therefore receive no guarantee that the information you buy is infallible.

In addition, criminals trying to sell cars with disguised identities, where the number and chassis plates have been swapped with another and a forged or false registration document obtained, are much more difficult to spot, and could fall though the HPI net.

> The HPI Autodata service can be bought over the telephone – (0722) 422422 – from Monday to Saturday between 8 am and 8 pm. The cost is £15 via Access, Visa or Mastercard. You can also write, enclosing a cheque for £15 payable to HPI Autodata, to HPI Information plc, Dolphin House, PO Box 61, New Street, Salisbury, Wiltshire SPI 2TB.

Used-car inspections

Few car buyers feel confident that they can discover for themselves the faults in a used car being offered for sale. They get around this by choosing to buy from a reputable garage, looking for a good guarantee or trusting to luck. You can, however, for a fee, get a car professionally inspected by one of the motoring organisations or an independent mechanic or garage, which should give you much more reassurance about its condition.

The concept of the used-car inspection is simple. You narrow down your choice of used car to the point where you are ready to buy it as long as it is mechanically satisfactory. You then call in an inspector who will give the car a thorough going-over. You will get a comprehensive written report on the condition of the car as well as some guidance on whether or not you should buy it.

Automobile Association (AA)

The motoring organisations are the main operators in this field, though there are many individual mechanics who advertise their services locally. The cost of the AA's Vehicle Inspection Report varies according to the size and complexity of the car, from £95 for a Metro, Nova or Fiesta to £237 for a Jaguar XJS, Rolls-Royce or BMW 7 Series. Non-members pay around 18 per cent more. The AA's contact number is (0345) 500610.

A number of garages buy in the AA inspections before the car is offered for sale, covering the cost themselves. The AA Car Check sign on a car on a dealer's forecourt means that it has been inspected to exactly the same standards as the individual test you would buy privately. That means the dealer will have the written AA report for you to study before you make up your mind, and you will be able to negotiate on points gleaned from the report which you feel justify a reduction in price.

The AA offers a second tier of service – Elite Vehicle Inspections – aimed at more complicated and consequently more expensive cars, which checks for faults in sophisticated components like the anti-lock braking system, four-wheel-drive and engine management systems. The inspection even includes a measurement of the thickness of the paint to highlight hidden bodywork defects and an HPI check.

Royal Automobile Club (RAC)

The RAC's vehicle examination scheme is fundamentally the same as the AA's ordinary inspection, but because cars are categorised by engine capacity rather than size, it is possible with some cars to make some significant savings over the AA's rates. The RAC's contact number is (0800) 333660.

Independent inspections

Any mechanic, competent or not, can set himself up as a 'used-vehicle inspector'. While the cost may appear attractive compared with that of the AA and RAC, the quality of the inspection will vary according to the diligence and experience of the individual operator. In many circumstances, therefore, it may be wiser to select one of the motoring organisations, unless you have been recommended to an independent inspector.

The real strength of the independent lies in areas where he has special expertise. If, for example, you have found a Citroën CX, then a mechanic with years of specialist experience with

Citroëns could be worth his weight in gold. That is equally true when it comes to exotic or classic cars, where depth of knowledge is all important.

How quick?

Fast response is vital for a car inspection. If everything about the car looks right, you do not want to risk losing it to another buyer because you have to wait days for the inspection to take place. Both the AA and RAC hope to get to most cars within a couple of days of a call. It can be much quicker – the same day – or, if there is a rush, it could take longer. You will be given a firm indication when you make your booking.

How is the seller going to react to an inspection?

Much will depend on the car being sold, and the reaction to the advertising. Understandably, if the telephone has not stopped ringing from the moment the used car was advertised, the seller may be reluctant to wait for a couple of days for your inspector to arrive. On the other hand, sellers trying to pull a fast one are going to react in just the same way, trying to push you into buying a less-than-perfect car by suggesting that there are lots of others after it. Watch out too for dealers who take offence, because you are suggesting that they might be trying to sell you a rogue car. That might well be the case.

Garages which are members of the Retail Motor Industry Federation should make no objections to an inspection. Part of the RMIF code of practice states that a dealer should go through a standard checklist and display it on the car. That gives the customer a reasonable idea of the condition of the car and also a form of cast-iron evidence should things go wrong. Unfortunately, but not surprisingly, this scheme has not been adopted everywhere.

THE MOT

Isn't a brand-new MOT certificate, valid for 12 months, a good sign that the car is generally OK? Unfortunately not. The MOT test is designed to test just two things: that the car is safe, and that its pollution levels are within limits. That means it tells you absolutely nothing about the mechanical condition of large areas of the car – the engine and gearbox, for example, will not be given a second thought. Also, the criminally minded will be able to organise their own MOT certificate on a really dodgy car. Even if a car has passed its MOT test the day before you see it, there is no guarantee that it is free of faults. (See Chapter 5 for full details on the MOT test.)

CHECKING A CAR YOURSELF

Many used-car buyers feel that their knowledge and experience, combined with a bit of common sense, will see them through when they make an inspection. That policy can work well as long as you are methodical about your approach – even the most organised person can get excited about the prospect of picking up a bargain and miss a vital point which costs him or her dear later.

If, however, you approach a car inspection in a logical manner, you could uncover potentially serious faults early on, and so not waste your time. The diagram opposite will help you pinpoint problem areas for rust.

Checking underneath for rust

The most serious form of corrosion will be found underneath the car. It is here that rust, when it gets a firm hold, will eventually signal the end of the life of the car, so it is important to check this area carefully. If you are buying from a garage, get it to put the car up on a lift so you can inspect the vehicle easily. If you are dealing with a private seller, putting the car up on a pair of ramps will be useful. *You must never rely on a car jack.* If you cannot get a car up on a hoist or ramps, you will simply have to rely on what you can check from the side of the car.

Types of rust

While you are inspecting, you will need to judge severity of damage. Surface rust on a flattish panel is the sort of thing you can sandpaper off with no bother. Flaky rust is not so easy to

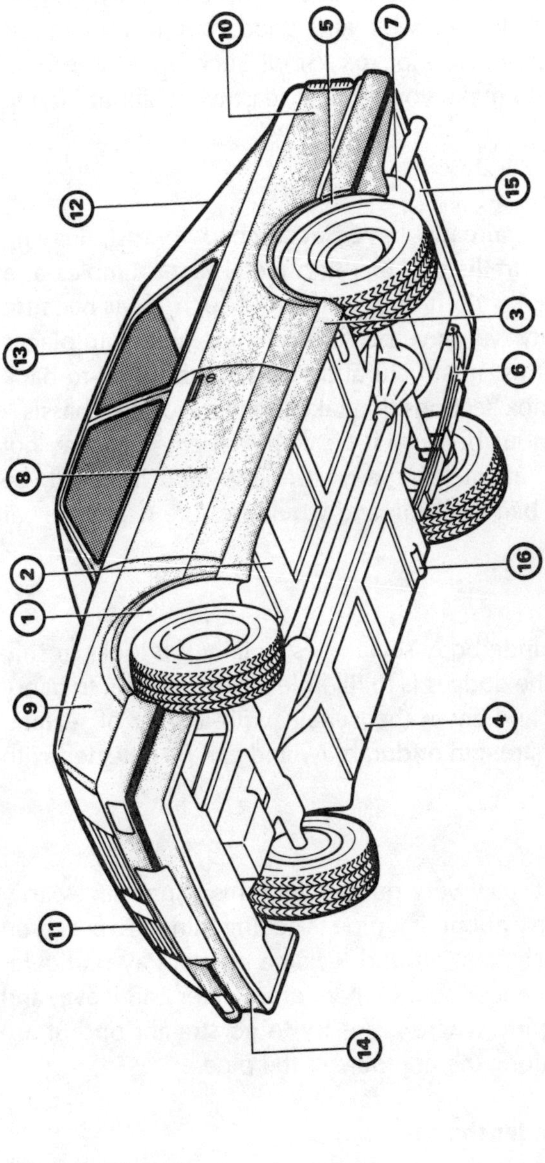

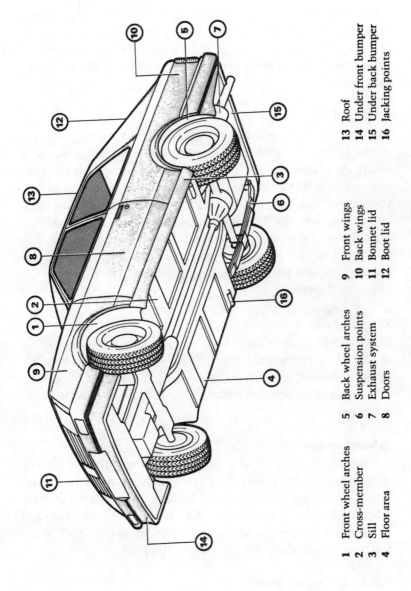

1 Front wheel arches
2 Cross-member
3 Sill
4 Floor area
5 Back wheel arches
6 Suspension points
7 Exhaust system
8 Doors
9 Front wings
10 Back wings
11 Bonnet lid
12 Boot lid
13 Roof
14 Under front bumper
15 Under back bumper
16 Jacking points

judge, and that is where the screwdriver test comes in. Select an accessible area, lay the blade almost flat on the rusty panel and scrub it vigorously to and fro. If the rust flakes off readily, leaving bright metal beneath, all well and good, but if you go on revealing successive layers of rust, *stop*! Such areas of rust, if widespread, should make you think at least twice about buying the car at all.

Structural rust

Some places may already have succumbed to rust, leaving visible holes, or a trellis of paper-thin metal that crumbles at a touch. As a general rule it is best to avoid such a car because rust of that severity will have been developing quietly in places you cannot see. Rust in structural members – the front-to-back and side-to-side box sections that take the place of the chassis – is particularly serious because it weakens the car. This may not be sufficient to affect everyday running, but it could be catastrophic in a bad collision and would be sure to fail the car in an MOT test.

Disguised rust

Beware of thick underbody sealant, especially if it looks freshly applied. One of the dodges is to fill holes with anything to hand, even cardboard, and cover the 'repair' with a layer of sealant. This provides no strength or durability and can be detected with a magnet.

Exhaust system

Exhaust pipes get rusty very quickly and this is not necessarily something to worry about. If a pipe is getting thin, however, you may find a greyish stain around leakage points. Pay particular attention to the silencer boxes where pipes enter and leave, and to bends in the pipe where gases try to go straight on but are forced to travel along the contours of the pipe.

While you are under the car

Look around the underside of the engine, gearbox, clutch housing and, on a rear-wheel-drive car, the back axle and differential, for signs of oil leaks. Check, too, brake pipes, and particularly unions, for signs of brake fluid leaks.

Checking on top

If the paintwork on a car has been neglected, rust can work its way through the metal. But often, rust eats through the metal the other way round, corroding from the underside of the panel. The first appearance it makes is a bubbling of the paintwork on the surface, by which time the true extent of the damage, and the cost of repairing it, can be substantial.

So check every panel of the car very carefully for signs of corrosion. Unfortunately, every car is prone to stone chipping along the front of the bonnet. A conscientious owner will have touched in these tiny chips with paint of the correct colour, so you should not dismiss a car automatically which has signs of attention in this area.

Accident damage

Accident damage, on the other hand, needs careful consideration. Even a minor dent can be a starting place for rust if the paint film is damaged sufficiently to let water get at the metal. Some paint films are tenacious enough to withstand minor impact and deformation, but others are more brittle and crack off. Look carefully along all the panels for the tell-tale ripples of repaired accident damage; stand back and view the car for colour mismatch; close in and look for overspray on parts that should not be coloured – window surrounds, bumpers, for example – and for small colour differences between panels.

Number plates

The number plates should tally and be the same as on the Vehicle Registration Document and tax disc. It is an obvious point, but you should be highly suspicious if there is any discrepancy.

Doors

Check that they all open, close and lock and fit properly – if not, it is a possible sign of crash damage.

Bumpers

Check that they do not look out-of-line in relation to the bodywork – another sign that the car may have hit something. And while you are down in that area, look under the bumper – often a neglected area, where rust can develop.

Dampness, tools

Check rubber seals around windows, doors, boot and bonnet for perishing and splits. Open the boot. Lift the boot lining and check for damp and rust – a sign of a poorly fitting lid or seals. Get any tools out of the boot – the car should certainly have a jack and wheel-changing gear, possibly more. Check with the seller that these are included with the sale.

Weak body

Jack the car up at each of its jacking points so that the wheels leave the ground. Does the bodywork around the jacking points show any sign of giving way or buckling when the car is lifted? Do the doors jam once the car is lifted? If so, you may be buying a lot of trouble if you go ahead with the deal.

Bearings

With the wheels still off the ground, grasp each wheel in turn at the top and bottom and see if you can rock it. Then try this from side to side. Free play indicates wear in bearings or steering and suspension joints.

Tyres

While you are down at each wheel examine the tyre for splits, bulges, cuts and uneven wear, and estimate whether the tyres will need replacing soon or not using your tread-depth gauge. If the tread depth is near 2mm you will have to buy new tyres almost immediately. Remember to check the spare tyre too.

Lights

With the car back down on the ground, a quick check of its lights is worthwhile. Ask the seller, or your companion, to sit in the car, turn the ignition on (but not start the engine) and work the switches, indicators and brake pedal; if the car has reversing lights, put it into reverse and check that they work.

Suspension

Check the car's dampers or shock absorbers by pushing down firmly on each corner of the car and then letting go – the car should bounce up and return immediately to its normal position. If it bounces a few times the damper or shock absorber needs replacing.

Under the bonnet

Probably, but misguidedly, people worry more about the state of a car's engine than anything else. In fact engines are, on average, pretty reliable.

You cannot tell much about the engine just by looking at it, but there are plenty of clues under the bonnet as to how much servicing care a car has had, and you can learn about the car's cooling system and electrics too. Most checks are a matter of simple observation.

Oil

Remove the dipstick and look at the colour of the oil, then do the same with the oil filler cap on top of the engine. If the oil is creamy brown, rather than black, it is likely that the engine has serious problems, perhaps a blown head gasket or worse.

Cooling system

Check for perished hoses and leaks. Make sure that no water is dripping from the radiator, and that the level of water in the radiator is full or almost full (*never open the radiator cap when the engine is hot*). A blown head gasket can also show up in the cooling water, so look for that creamy, oil mixture instead of clear fluid.

Engine

Look for leaks around the engine and then start it up. Engines are rarely quiet, but if it makes strange noises or has a very smoky exhaust, tread carefully.

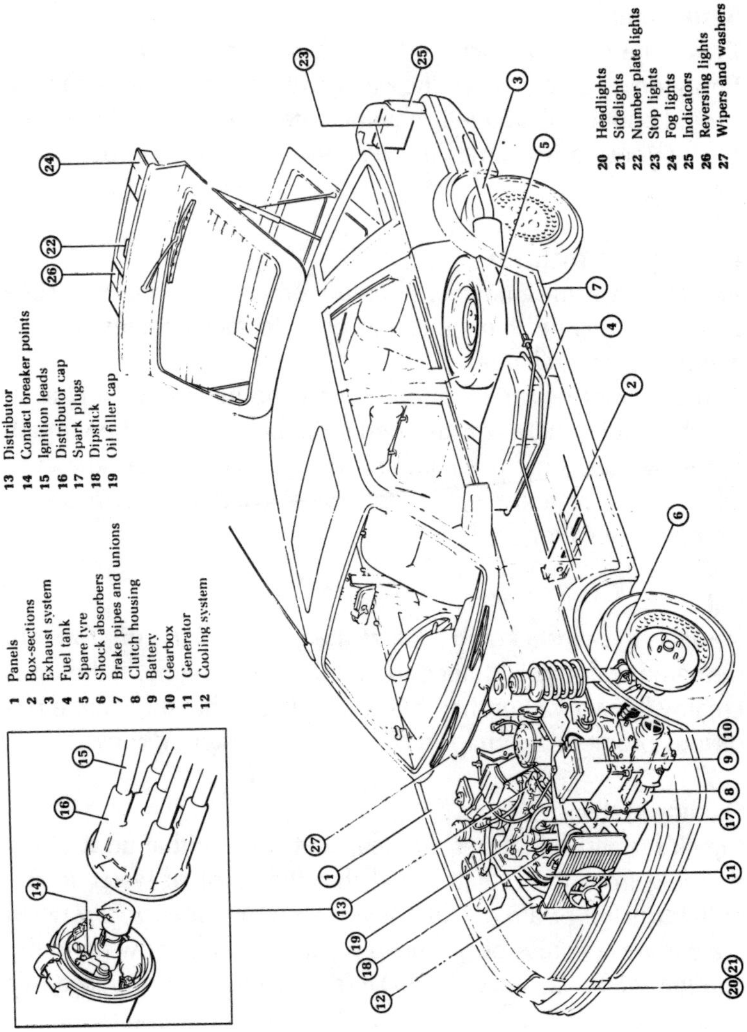

1 Panels
2 Box-sections
3 Exhaust system
4 Fuel tank
5 Spare tyre
6 Shock absorbers
7 Brake pipes and unions
8 Clutch housing
9 Battery
10 Gearbox
11 Generator
12 Cooling system
13 Distributor
14 Contact breaker points
15 Ignition leads
16 Distributor cap
17 Spark plugs
18 Dipstick
19 Oil filler cap
20 Headlights
21 Sidelights
22 Number plate lights
23 Stop lights
24 Fog lights
25 Indicators
26 Reversing lights
27 Wipers and washers

Inside the car

Now you have gone through the major mechanical and bodywork checks you can get on with the more straightforward matter of the state of the inside of the car. Unless you are already familiar with the model, you will probably find yourself absorbed by the novelty of an 'unknown' car. Try to remain objective: maybe the seats, the radio or the controls are terrific, but do not allow your judgement to be distorted by appealing features and goodies.

Steering

You can check for steering play in non power-assisted-steering cars by standing by the open driver's window and watching the front wheels while you turn the steering wheel – there should be no more than an inch movement of your hand on the rim before the road wheels start to move. For power-assisted steering, wait until the road test to do checks.

Electrics

Now is the time to check that the electrical items all work correctly. You should have already gone over the lights, so now operate the wipers and washers (both front and back), the heater fan, interior lights, and the radio/cassette, as well as any other bits and pieces. Remember you will probably have to switch the ignition on before some of these will operate, but there is no need to actually start the engine.

Trim

Many of the problems with interior trim and fittings are simply to do with heavy or careless use. They may not actually stop the car working as it should and you can decide for yourself just how smart you would like a car to be. If trim is damaged it can be surprisingly awkward and expensive to replace. Finally, lift the carpets if you can. If you discover severe rust underneath, forget the car.

The road test

The final stage of your appraisal is the road test. It is important that you, as a prospective buyer, get to drive the car before you make your buying decision. If you do not you run the risk of being fooled by a seller who knows how to 'drive around' the car's faults, as well as finding out too late that you do not actually like the way the car drives. As long as you have some experience as a driver you will no doubt soon spot any serious problems that affect the control and response of the car. Here are a few points to remember as you do your checks.

Starting the engine

This is important. It is best to evaluate starting with a cold engine, but you may well find that the engine is warm when you arrive to carry out the inspection. Whatever the temperature, an engine which proves reluctant to start is unlikely to get any easier once you have bought it. The problem could be minor or major – only an experienced mechanic will be able to tell.

Gearchange

Some cars have inherently poor gear selection, so a poor gearchange may not actually indicate a fault. You should, however, consider whether a mediocre gearchange is something with which you can live.

Brakes

When carrying out checks on brakes, check behind you *and* warn any passengers in the car that you are going to brake. Braking problems obviously have serious safety implications but generally are not very difficult to resolve. If you cannot test the handbrake on a hill, do not worry – problems are usually a matter of adjustment and are not too expensive to remedy.

Clutch

Clutches wear and need replacing in the routine course of events, but they are expensive none the less. On a clear road put the car in fourth gear at 40 mph and press the accelerator firmly to the floor. Repeat the process in third gear. If the engine speed rises sharply, without the car accelerating as you would expect, the clutch probably needs replacing.

Engine

Engines vary enormously: some are clattery, some do not idle smoothly, some are very noisy. The clearest signs of serious engine trouble are low oil pressure and the colour of the exhaust gases. Check that the oil pressure warning light in the instrument panel doesn't come on when the engine is idling. Every car has such a warning light. Unscrupulous sellers have been known to disconnect them. To check this, turn the ignition switch on but do not start the engine – the oil pressure warning switch must then glow.

Blue smoke indicates wear in piston rings or cylinders and will involve the replacement of parts, or possibly the whole engine; either option is to be avoided. Black smoke indicates a clogged air filter or an overly rich fuel mixture.

Steering

Check that the steering is not too heavy for you, particularly when parking. Steering vibration is rarely a major fault. Often, simple wheel balancing will correct any problem. If there is a more serious problem, like pulling to one side or a permanent instability, it could prove costly to correct, so get a second opinion.

After the road test

There are still a few checks to do after you have gone on your road test. You should have driven the car enough to get it thoroughly warm. Only then will you be able to tell about certain aspects, particularly to do with the engine.

Remove the oil filler cap and check for smoke or fumes. These indicate wear in piston rings or cylinders. You may have to replace parts, or at worst get a new engine.

Check the oil pressure gauge, if one is fitted. If the pressure is low when the engine is idling, the oil pump could be faulty or the engine worn. The pump will need replacing and the engine may need to be overhauled or even replaced.

Press the accelerator quickly from idle and listen for:

- engine knocking noise indicating worn bearings which will involve an overhaul of the engine

- a squeal or screech which could be caused by a loose drive belt or worn water pump – parts will need to be checked and possibly replaced
- excessive clatter, indicating worn valve gear – parts will need to be replaced.

If the engine is idling poorly or too fast, this could be a sign that the engine needs retuning.

CHAPTER 3

SELLING A CAR

HOW TO SELL YOUR OLD CAR

You have plenty of choice in the way you sell your old car. Some options are easy, others take time and effort. Unfortunately, the easy option is rarely the one which nets you the best possible price.

Going back to basics, you have two real choices. The first is to go to a dealer and part exchange your old car for its replacement. The other is to sell your car yourself and buy the replacement outright. Both methods have their strengths and weaknesses, and only you can really decide how the pros and cons add up.

Part exchange

There can be little doubt that part exchanging your existing car for the next one is the easiest solution. If all goes according to plan, the dealer will buy your car from you at the same time as you buy your new one from him. All that has to be done is to make up the difference in value between the two cars – invariably that money seems to flow in the direction of the car dealer.

The big advantage of this option is that so little hassle is involved. Once you have agreed to the deal in principle, there is merely the matter of turning up at the appointed time, dealing with the paperwork, handing over your keys, picking up the new ones and driving off. You have no awkward period when you own two cars, or none at all, no expenses for advertising your car for sale, and no time is wasted dealing with potential buyers who change their minds. There are fewer risks, both from the personal safety and financial side, and you get no telephone calls from agents pestering you to advertise in their magazine or paper.

So why doesn't everyone part exchange? Simply because the money a dealer will pay for your car (or 'allow you' in dealer-speak) is usually less than you could get if you sold the car privately. The reasons for this are pretty obvious: the dealer has overheads to meet, will probably need to offer a guarantee on your car and, of course, would like to make as much profit as possible.

That is why it is tempting to cut out the middle man and sell the car yourself. The easy mistake to make is thinking that you can sell your car for the same price you see advertised on a dealer's forecourt. If *you* had the choice between two identical cars, one from a dealer, the other at the same price advertised privately, where would you go? To the dealer, who will probably see you at your convenience, who will have insurance cover when you take a test drive, who will surely offer you some form of warranty in the price, and can offer help with finance and probably insurance too if you need it. Most dealers will even find a used car to your liking if they have not got one in stock. In contrast the private seller can offer none of these benefits, so the price he or she asks should reasonably be lower.

Finally, do not expect a dealer to discuss the nitty-gritty of part exchange values if he has not seen your car. Take it with you when you go to look at the one you want to buy, so the dealer can give it a look-over and make a binding offer. If you do not, at best you will receive a 'yes we might be interested' response – certainly no self-respecting salesman would attempt to value a part exchange he or she has not seen first-hand.

Selling privately

If you choose to sell your car privately you should, in most circumstances, achieve a better price than you would get either part exchanging it for another, or even selling directly to a dealer who is keen enough on your car to buy it without selling you another. You have a wide range of options from which to choose.

Classified ads

The favourite method for the private sale is the classified ad. Here, in a matter of a few lines of purple prose, you describe your car to its best advantage, take a stab at its value, drop in a telephone number and wait for the telephone to start ringing.

The choice of outlets for your classified advertisement is enormous, so it is important to select with care. If your car is a prestige or exotic model, you may find a publication which offers nationwide coverage gives the best results – *The Sunday Times* is the market leader in this field. The cost is relatively high, however, and you are unlikely to place an attractive advertisement for under £50 for a single insertion.

At the other end of the scale is the local newspaper. This is a better bet for cheaper cars, where few buyers will be prepared to travel long distances in order to make a purchase. As many towns support several local papers it is a good idea to study them all and then choose the one which seems to support the most *private* car advertising. There is little point in picking the cheapest paper only to find your advertisement is lost among more prominent display adverts from dealers.

There is an increasing number of free-advertising newspapers, such as *Loot*, which operate either regionally or concentrate on a local area. Generally these cover a whole range of items, from washing machines to houses. You pay nothing for the ad, so it is an opportunity well worth taking.

Somewhere between the national and local newspapers fall the classified car advertising magazines, of which *Auto Trader* and *Exchange and Mart* are the biggest sellers. *Auto Trader* comes in a dozen regional issues, so the coverage is localised to an extent. The fee of around £16 includes a photograph of your car, taken by a local agent. *Exchange and Mart* is divided into two regions, north and south, and charges around £1 per word. Both of these publications sell weekly in large numbers and seem to offer a successful method of selling.

Once you have advertised your car in any of the publications mentioned above, it is highly likely that your telephone will ring in response. Unfortunately, there will not always be an interested buyer on the other end of the line, but instead a telephone salesman canvassing you to advertise your car in another publication. It is probably best not to take up one of these offers until you have at least seen the publication they are promoting and judged whether the type of advertising really suits the car you are trying to sell. Ask about prices early on in the conversation, too, as these can be very high.

Auctions

Putting your car through an auction will almost ensure you of a sale. The procedure is very straightforward. Contact a nearby car auction company to find out the times and dates of forthcoming auctions (look in the *Yellow Pages* or *Thomson* under Car Auctions). While most auctions started up as locations for traders to buy and sell cars, and still get most of their business this way, many will be able to provide plenty of guidance to private sellers.

You will be told when and where to bring your car, and you should ask for an explanation of the fee structure and when the proceeds of the sale will be handed over. The cost of selling through an auction is high, perhaps 10 per cent of the hammer price, plus VAT. It is the price you pay to get a quick sale.

Unless your car is in the banger category, the auctioneers will allow you to put a 'reserve' figure on it. This is its minimum value to you. If the bids do not reach this level, the car will not be sold, and it will be auctioned again at the next sale. That may sound good, but bids made at auctions tend to be low, rarely reaching much more than the 'trade' price. It is quite likely that the auctioneers will not let you name what they consider to be an unrealistically high reserve because it would waste everyone's time. Auctions are good for selling cars fast, not for getting high prices.

Computer bureaux and brokers

In recent years a number of companies have been offering a form of 'computer dating', claiming to match your car to potential buyers who have registered with them. The seller pays a fee and then waits to be contacted by buyers on the bureaux' lists. This method of selling relies upon the seller placing complete trust in the integrity of the bureau as, unlike published magazines which are there for everyone to see and buy, you have to act in good faith that the bureau really does have lists of potential buyers looking for a car like yours. On balance, there are more reassuring methods of selling a used car.

Car marts

The idea behind these is that you arrive at the mart first thing on a weekend or bank holiday morning, pay perhaps £15 to park your car and then wait for potential buyers to turn up – a car boot sale where you sell the car as well. It is not a bad idea, though the through-put of genuine buyers may not be all it seems. Before you take this path, it might be a good idea to make a visit to a mart and talk to other sellers to judge the level of interest they have experienced.

Owners' clubs

Advertising in an owners' club magazine will ensure that you reach the people who are most enthusiastic about your type of car. These clubs tend to be confined to cars which are classics or potential classics.

Shop windows

An advertisement on a postcard placed in a local shop window should cost well under a pound a week and can bring a surprising amount of exposure. There is much to be said for this method of selling, especially if you are asking less than £1,000 and are not in a rush to sell.

Car window sign

The biggest mistake owners make when they put a 'For Sale' sign in their car window is that passers-by cannot read it at a glance. The sign needs to be BIG, written with a thick black marker pen so the message really stands out. It can work, too, and costs you nothing.

Passing the word around

Tell your friends and neighbours you want to sell your car. People love buying a car from someone they, or a friend, know. But remember that friendships may depend upon the car you are selling not having any hidden faults.

Selling to the trade

Some dealers will buy your car outright, without any need for part exchange. They will always ask you how much you are looking for, so have a good idea before you start talking, and be prepared to be flexible. Do not give up in despair and accept a low price just because the first dealer says your car is no good – ask others.

You need to select the dealers you visit with care. Garages selling brand-new cars are likely to be most interested in buying cars of the same make, up to 3 years old. So if your car does not fall into this category, look for a dealer who seems to specialise in your make or model of car, or go to a garage which concentrates on used cars. With luck, and a bit of homework on used-car values, you could get the same figure that your car would fetch at an auction without having to worry about the commission.

SETTING THE PRICE

How much is your second-hand car worth? It is important to get this figure right in your own mind at an early stage so that you neither sell it too cheaply, nor find that no one shows any interest because you are expecting too much.

Valuing a used car is never easy. Take any car of a certain age, and there will be a nominal value which then has to be adjusted to account for a number of other factors. The mileage the car has covered, its condition, the registration letter, the time of year – each can push the nominal value up or down by hundreds of pounds.

Car dealers will use *Glass's Guide* or the *CAP Black Book* to give them the basic guidelines on a car's worth, which they will then adjust to suit their own experience and circumstances.

Neither *Glass*'s nor *CAP* are available to the general public, but a number of used-car price guides can be bought at newsagents, while many motoring magazines, like *Auto Express*, give a more limited listing of used values on a regular basis.

Like the car dealers, you will need to take the 'guide' values as a starting point rather than as the final figure. You will, anyway, almost certainly be confronted by a choice of values.

The forecourt or retail price

This is the figure a dealer will start off with when he advertises a car for sale. It is the highest possible value of the car, and is not a figure you should hope to attain by selling the car privately.

The trade price

There are several slightly different interpretations of the trade price of a used car, but generally it is the value of the car to a motor trader or dealer. The trade price is significantly less than the forecourt price, to allow for the cost of the dealer running his business and for the profit margin. It will be the starting point a dealer uses when he is assessing the value of your car in part exchange for another.

Auction price

This is the price a car will fetch at auction. By and large it should be similar to the trade price, as buyers at auction are largely traders. But the auction price can be higher than trade, or, more likely, lower.

Private sale price

This is the value you might get for your car if you sold it to a private buyer. It is not quoted in every guide to used-car prices, but if you pitch midway between retail and trade values you will arrive at a fair starting point for a private sale.

Unless you have all the time in the world, it does not pay to be greedy deciding what you want for your car. If you advertise it for sale privately, you will be competing with many other people trying to do the same thing. The final adjustments in your advertised price should be made by looking through as many private car advertisements as you can find. Above all, you need to be competitive with these prices, do not go in at a higher figure unless you have a convincing reason to do so. Any car will sell if the price is right, so if your telephone does not ring, the most likely reason is that you are asking too much.

FACTORS WHICH AFFECT THE VALUE OF YOUR SECOND-HAND CAR

Even when you have arrived at what you feel genuinely is a reasonable price for your car, there will be influences which may force you to think again.

Registration letter Cars registered after 1 August, with the newer letter on the number plate, are always worth more (typically £100 to £500, depending upon the model and its age).

Mileage The 'average' mileage is 10,000 to 12,000 annually for the first two or three years, then it drops back to 8,000 to 10,000 per year. Much more or less than this will have a marked affect on the value.

Time of year In the spring and early summer, and in September, used values are generally at their best. The depths of winter are generally a bad time to get the best price on a used car unless it has four-wheel-drive.

Body variant Convertibles are worth much more in the spring and early summer. Big-bodied 4x4s fetch their best prices in the autumn and winter. Hatchback versions of family cars usually fetch a bit more than saloons, owing to their greater practicality.

Size of car With a few exceptions, it is always easier to sell smaller cars than larger ones, so the prices tend to be strongest for Fiesta- and Escort-sized cars, then progressively weaken through Sierras and Granadas. It is easy to find 6-year-old Granadas selling at the same price as 6-year-old Fiestas.

Colour Good strong colours make a difference. Metallics and bright red fetch the best prices, black and white are not too bad, but buyers seem to steer away from blues, browns and beiges unless the price is attractive.

Engine Diesel cars have traditionally been worth more than petrol versions. Though this may change as more used diesels become available, high-mileage diesels are always likely to fetch a better price than petrol cars with a similar mileage reading. Big-engined versions of any car often fall in value more quickly than the lower-capacity models.

Gearbox Automatic transmission is considered almost a necessity on luxury models like Mercedes-Benz, Jaguar and BMW. Though these cars are produced in manual gearbox versions, they are usually worth significantly less. Cars of the Vauxhall Carlton and Senator size with the biggest engines also fetch better prices as automatics, but manuals are as popular in the two-litre size. Medium and small cars with an automatic gearbox may fetch better prices when they are relatively new, but then fall to the level of the manual versions, or even below.

Optional extras The value of a used car is firmly linked to the specification of the precise model – L, GL or Ghia, for example. Very little account seems to be taken of any optional extras, which can be a big disappointment for the original purchaser when the time comes to sell. Astonishingly, the value of items like air-conditioning, anti-lock brakes or leather interior falls to a quarter of its original cost after only a year, and can be almost worthless after that except as an added inducement to buy.

PREPARING YOUR CAR FOR SALE

It is important that your car is at its best when potential buyers come to inspect it. A simple wash and vacuum may do the trick, but it is more likely that it will take two or three hours to get it looking pristine.

The outside

The first impression that a buyer gets of your car will be very important. Quite possibly, after the arrangements have been made over the telephone for a visit, a potential private purchaser will take a quick look at your car before even knocking on your door. If your car looks tatty, you have lost that sale straight away. Dealers, too, know that no matter how good the car is mechanically, the initial appearance will be very important to their customers. So if the car does not look right, the dealer will have to spend money to get it in shape.

Your first step in preparation is to attack the paintwork. Clean the car with soap and water, and then leather it dry. If there are stubborn spots of tar or bird droppings, you might try a common decorating solvent, such as white spirit, or buy a special cleaner from a car accessory shop.

Next touch in the paint chips. These are almost inevitable on cars more than a few years old, and are usually concentrated along the front of the bonnet and the back edges of the doors. The safest option is to buy the correct colour touch-up paint, complete with brush, from your car dealer, though car accessory shops stock a range of the most common finishes. Touching in small paint blemishes is a very straightforward job, the key being to use as little paint as possible so that the repair hardly shows. *Do not* get carried away with the idea of spraying paint over damage unless you are experienced – it really is very difficult to get an acceptable finish.

Then you should apply some polish to the paintwork, though if the appearance is very dull your time may be better spent using a paint restorer. This contains an abrasive which removes the dull top layer of paint to reveal the fresher finish below, and can be used on most types of paintwork, including metallic which has a very hard lacquer surface. If you have any doubts about your metallic paint, polish a small, discreet area first. If there is no sign of paint or a black discolouration from the metallic particles, then it has a lacquered surface.

Strictly speaking, you should then use a polish to protect the fresh paint you have exposed, although the shine will remain for a good few weeks after you have treated it. If you have not used an abrasive cleaner, an hour spent with a conventional polish will improve the appearance of almost every car. Finish off by cleaning the wheels and the black plastic parts. Again, special products are available from accessory shops and, particularly with alloy wheels, these do the job far better than you could hope to achieve with a soapy sponge.

The inside

Sprucing up the inside of the car can be more difficult than dealing with the outside. Carpets and seats need to be vacuumed, the dashboard and plastic parts cleaned and lolly wrappers and dog hair removed. Smokers should empty and wash out the ashtrays, and then fumigate the interior to avoid putting off the large body of non-smokers who will walk away at the first whiff of stale cigarette smoke. Attack stains on seats with a proprietary cleaner, and make sure the inside of the glass gets attention.

Getting the job done for you

If this all seems like too much effort, plenty of car valet companies will do the job for you. The charges can vary between £10 and £50, depending upon the size of your car and the level of cleaning you require. A top-price service should offer exterior cleaning, waxing, engine bay clean, interior vacuuming and shampoo. As the cleaning agents and equipment are likely to be better than those you use yourself, the finished job should be better, too.

DEALING WITH PRIVATE BUYERS

For many of us the thought of selling a car privately is not a particularly enticing prospect, yet, spurred on by the thought that we should be a few hundred pounds better off than if we part exchanged, we go through the motions with trepidation. If you approach the matter systematically, however, the whole business can go like clockwork.

Handling telephone calls

The first rule is to be helpful and polite to inquirers. That may demand a little patience, as some potential buyers will be as nervous about the whole affair as you might be. The end result can be a stream of questions on features you have already spelt out in your advertisement. You should, therefore, have a few additional selling points up your sleeve to ice the cake – the fact you have owned the car for several years, that it has always been regularly serviced and you have all the old garage bills will please a potential buyer and encourage him or her to move to the next step, coming to see the car.

Do not, however, 'oversell' the car. There is nothing more irritating for a buyer than to make a journey to see a car which is nothing like as attractive as you have made out. It wastes the buyer's time and, in the end, yours too if he or she turns away from the purchase. A degree of openness about a car's faults and weaknesses at the telephone stage can convince a buyer that you are being honest and therefore a person worth dealing with. Unfortunately, you may get some time-wasters. Those who waste your time on the telephone are merely irritating, but the ones that make arrangements and then do not arrive are more annoying.

Making appointments to view

You should make appointments for callers to inspect your car during the daylight hours. In winter that will probably restrict you to the weekends and therefore force you into 'booking in' callers that show interest mid-week. No matter how enthusiastic a potential buyer sounds on the telephone, you should avoid giving him or her 'first refusal' if he or she cannot come to see the car as soon as is convenient to you. If, for example, a buyer cannot view your car before Sunday, you stand the chance of losing potential sales from later callers who could come on the Saturday. Be realistic, and try to tempt buyers along without accepting them as the number one candidate. If you do, and a buyer turns up at the appointed time to find the car has been sold to someone else, he or she could be very angry indeed.

Discouraging undesirables

Everyone has to be wary of undesirable visitors. Women especially should always make sure that their car is viewed in broad daylight, and should never travel elsewhere to demonstrate a car. A visible companion is a good idea. Getting prospective visitors to leave a telephone number where they can be contacted helps the feeling of security. Better still, insist on the telephone number being a permanent one, not a mobile, and then call it back to check it out – refuse to see the buyer if everything does not add up.

Handling the test drive

Most potential buyers will rightly want to test drive the car before making a final decision. You, as the seller, should be wary of two things. First, the buyer might be a thief who will disappear on the test drive never to return. Second, the buyer may not have adequate insurance cover.

So you need to take some precautions. *Never* allow a test drive without you or a friend as a passenger; even keep the keys in your hand as you are swapping over seats. As for insurance, if your policy covers any driver, you are covered. If not, you will have to rely on the buyer's insurance, which may be legal but is unlikely to be comprehensive.

Most car insurance policies provide cover for the policyholder when driving another car not owned by him or her. This means that legally such a person may drive your car. What will not be covered, however, is any damage. You might get the buyer to sign a form before the test drive accepting responsibility for any damage – though, in reality, most sellers seem to chance it.

Professional inspections

A buyer may decide that he or she would like to have a professional inspection of the car. That is reasonable, but make sure he or she is truly interested in the car as you will have to put other potential buyers on hold for a couple of days until the inspection is complete. It is therefore fair to ask for a small returnable deposit as a sign of good faith. The inspector will doubtless want to drive the car – AA and RAC men can be trusted – and treat him as you would any buyer and go along for the ride.

Finalising the deal

Private buyers usually expect to haggle a bit, so you should be prepared for this and willing to drop a little from your advertised price. Once you have agreed on a figure, you will need a deposit to secure the car, unless the buyer has a pocket full of cash and can therefore take the car away immediately. You really should be asking for a minimum of £50 for cars costing under £1,000, and £100 to £200 for those above that. Cash is ideal for the deposit – a cheque can be cancelled unless covered by a high-value cheque card. Remember that once you have agreed a price and accepted the deposit, you are obliged to sell the car to this person, even if you get offered a better price later.

Handling the money

This is potentially a tricky time. Accepting cash for your car is straightforward, as long as the notes are not forged. Never hand over the keys after receiving a normal cheque until it has been cleared by your bank, which generally takes three working days. With a banker's draft or building society cheque you should telephone the issuing branch (written on the cheque) to confirm that the draft or cheque in your hand is a valid one. That cuts out Sundays as a change-over day, perhaps Saturdays too.

Paperwork

It is a legal requirement for you to fill out the slip at the bottom of the registration document and then send it off to the DVLC at Swansea, informing it of the change of owner. A buyer will also want the MOT certificate on cars over 3 years old, the handbook and service book, plus a receipt for the money paid to you for the car. If your car is on any form of finance, like hire purchase, it is probably not yours to sell as you choose. If that is the case, call the finance company for advice on the way to go about disposing of the car and settling your outstanding loan.

CHAPTER 4

RUNNING AND SERVICING A CAR

Three major elements are involved in the cost of running a car. Depreciation (covered in Chapter 1) is a measure of the way a car loses value between the time you buy it and the time you come to sell. Then there is the money tied up in the car, which is unavoidable. If you borrow the money to buy, you will end up paying interest to the lender. If you already have sufficient cash, then you will lose the opportunity to earn investment income when you withdraw it from savings. Finally there are the running costs. These are made up of the cost of everything else – fuel, servicing, repairs and routine replacements, for example. Insurance is also a part, though this is such a big subject that it is dealt with separately in Chapter 6.

HOW RUNNING COSTS BUILD UP

The day-to-day running cost is the price of motoring most immediately visible to the owner. You know each time you fill up with petrol and every time the car comes back from a service how much it is costing you, but it remains very easy to overlook the true cost over the year. To do that you need to log the following areas of expenditure.

Fuel

Your fuel bills, whether your car runs on petrol or diesel, are related not only to the mileage you cover but to how and where you drive. A sympathetic driver can readily achieve fuel consumption figures 25 per cent better than a press-on driver over the same route. And the route makes a big difference, too. Steady cruising at 50 mph will often halve the amount of petrol consumed compared with the same car used in stop-start town driving. Even worse, short school runs, where the car is driven for just a couple of miles from cold, can produced horrifying fuel consumption figures in many cars, especially those with large engines.

Road fund licence

Though there has been frequent talk of the road fund licence being abolished in favour of an increased taxation of fuel, this form of taxation appears to be well entrenched. The road fund licence must be paid for every car used on public roads, even if it is merely parked in the street. Your only say in the matter is whether you choose to pay the fee annually (£130 at the time of writing) or twice a year, for an additional 10 per cent premium.

MOT certificate

Once a car reaches three years of age it requires an MOT certificate (see Chapter 5); after that the requirement is annual. The certificate is given after the car has been inspected by an authorised garage. Most of the test is designed to assess whether the car is safe to use, though more recently the exhaust emissions have been included as well. Modern cars have very strict requirements for emissions, but older cars are allowed more leniency as many were designed before any form of emission legislation applied. At around £25 the test itself is reasonably priced, though the older a car gets, the more likely it is to need additional work – and thus expense – in order to comply.

Servicing

Every car has a service schedule which has been designed by the car manufacturer to ensure the car runs at its optimum and the components last as long as they should. When the car is supplied new it comes with a service book which outlines the service intervals and what is required. Most cars produced in the last 15 years need a service between every 6,000 and 12,000 miles, with the fall-back of a service once every 12 months if you cover a low mileage. The cost of a service varies greatly from garage to garage and car to car. Many owners of cars up to 3 years old go to a franchised dealer for their servicing; after that, there is a drift towards independent service outlets and finally to do-it-yourself servicing.

A perception persists among owners that servicing at the franchised dealer is more expensive than elsewhere, and is not really worth the trouble. There are, however, some strong reasons for remaining with a franchised dealer for your servicing (and repair) work. Every new car comes with a mechanical warranty which will last between one and three years, depending upon the model of car. The terms of this warranty almost certainly will require you to have your car serviced according to the precise schedule at an authorised dealer – not necessarily the one you bought the car from, but a dealer franchised for your make. If you do not follow these strict requirements, you may well find getting work done under the guarantee becomes more tricky.

A similar situation exists with long-term corrosion warranties, where many car manufacturers require you to return the car to the authorised dealer for an annual inspection. Though you are free to get your servicing carried out elsewhere, you may find the dealer charges you more for the annual inspection than if he had carried it out at the same time as the routine service.

Finally, there is the service history of the car. The second-hand value of prestige and specialist cars is particularly affected by whether they have been serviced correctly by their owner. By moving outside the official recognised network of dealers for your servicing, you may well find you lose a considerable amount of the potential resale value.

Routine replacements

All cars need certain parts replacing from time to time, not because they are faulty, but because they wear or become less efficient with use. Two obvious examples are tyres and the oil filter. The life of a tyre will vary according to a number of factors: the construction of the tyre (hard tyres last longer but do not grip so well, so different manufacturers arrive at different compromises), the way the car is driven, the tyre pressures and the correct adjustment of the steering, for example. The life of the same tyre will also vary from car to car – some cars are notoriously heavy on tyres because they have been designed to exploit all the grip available.

Additional items which you must expect to replace from time to time because they have worn out are brake pads and shoes, the clutch, and windscreen wiper blades. Shock absorbers (part of the suspension) may also need replacement after a few years, although as wear in this area is so tricky to spot, it is always worth getting a second opinion before you pay for this particular task to be carried out.

The other category of routine replacement includes filters, engine oil and spark plugs. These items get less efficient the longer they are in the car, and the manufacturer recommends that after a certain period they are replaced anew. This normally occurs at one of the routine services, which is why it is important to stick to the regular service schedule.

Repairs

The likely cost of repairs to a car is difficult to predict. You may choose a car which comes out as one of the most reliable in the *Which?* car reliability survey and be satisfied for several years, only to find that when something does go seriously wrong, the cost of fixing it is extremely expensive. On the other hand, a car which is inherently less reliable may have very cheap spares available at every car accessory shop, and so the main problem will be inconvenience rather than the cost of repair. Either way, it makes sense to budget for some repairs over a year. If you reckon on, say, £200 in addition to your servicing costs, you should not be too hard hit by the need for a few minor repairs or some routine replacements, like tyres.

HOW TO CHOOSE A CAR WHICH IS NOT GOING TO COST A FORTUNE TO RUN

Many motorists buy a car on the price and features, without seriously considering how much it will cost them in the long run to own and maintain. About as far as most people go is to consider the fuel consumption and the cost of insurance. So if you are planning things carefully from the outset, how do you make sure that the car you will buy is not going to ruin you in the years to come?

Engine size

There is some truth in the old adage: the bigger the engine the more fuel it will use. But technology has improved fuel consumption in more modern cars, which means that a 1,600cc car built today might return better mpg figures than a 1,300cc car designed 10 years earlier. A difficulty also occurs when a car manufacturer puts a small engine – 1,300cc or 1,400cc engine, say – into a family car, in order to offer a cheap model to tempt buyers into the range. It is quite feasible for these cars to provide adequate performance and good fuel economy with just a couple of people on board, but to suffer in both performance and economy compared with a 1,600cc model when fully loaded.

The best advice is to look at the government fuel consumption figures for the car you are interested in, or the figures in the annual *Which? Guide to New and Used Cars.*

Petrol versus diesel

Diesel engines use inherently less fuel than those run on petrol, and so will undoubtedly save you money in the long run. This is particularly true in town driving, where the differences are even more marked, while at motorway speeds the differential closes. Diesel fuel in the UK is usually priced very close to that of unleaded petrol, so there are no additional savings to be made, though in France you will find that diesel is approximately two-thirds the price of petrol.

There is also a commonly held belief that diesel engines will run for much greater distances than petrol engines before giving any trouble. As a consequence a keen market exists for diesels which have covered over 75,000 miles, but not for petrol-engined cars which have had the same amount of use.

A diesel car has its disadvantages. One is the engine noise, which despite many recent advances is uncommonly loud when starting from cold and is certain to be noticed by all around you on a chilly winter's morning. The performance can be poor compared with a petrol engine of similar size. Diesel engines with turbo-chargers are much better in this respect, and with their more flexible performance are preferred to petrol cars by some drivers, though the downside is that fuel economy is not quite as good as that achieved by a non-turbo diesel.

Diesel cars are generally more expensive to buy new. Until 1993, car manufacturers tended to charge a premium of anything between £400 and £800 for a diesel engine. With the increasing interest in diesel cars this differential in new car prices is fading away, while the value of *used* diesels is still higher than that of equivalent petrol cars.

Insurance

In recent years the cost of car insurance has increased sharply, which makes it particularly important to look at this aspect when choosing a replacement car. The way to do this is simple. Ask your current insurance company or broker for the classification, or rating, of your current car and the one you are thinking about. If the rating of your proposed car is higher, it will cost more to insure, if lower, then less.

All companies use a 20-point scale to classify cars, with a basic Mini in Group 1 and a Ferrari in 20. You can find the ratings for new cars in many motoring magazines, while used models are covered in the used-car price guides in newsagents.

Servicing costs

There can be vast differences in the cost of servicing cars, particularly if you stick to the network of franchised dealers. Some car manufacturers proudly promote their cars as cheap to service. Others see it as a way of increasing the profit levels for their dealers and require a great deal of work during routine servicing.

A simple check you can run is to telephone a dealer's service department and ask about the cost of intermediate and major services, as well as the intervals. This way you can spot a car which is costly to service before you commit yourself to buying it.

If you decide not to use the authorised dealers for servicing (bearing in mind the warnings given above), you will find a great many garages offer fixed-price deals no matter what the make of car. Remember, however, that the cost of any special parts which need replacing in addition to the service could well be close to that at the franchised dealer.

KEEPING YOUR RUNNING COSTS IN CHECK

Even after you have bought your car, and it turns out not to be the most economical to run, there are still ways to minimise your expenses.

Cheap fuel

The price of petrol and diesel fuel can vary by as much as seven pence per litre in the same town, equivalent to perhaps £3.50 on a tank-full in the average car. The most expensive places from which to buy are inevitably the forecourts of the big-name fuel companies, while supermarkets tend to be the cheapest. Should you worry about buying a supermarket own-brand in preference to one of the major brands?

Fuel has to comply with a number of British and European standard tests, so you can rest assured that the fuel you buy from any source will be suitable for your car. The major fuel companies, however, are now promoting the 'additives' included in their fuel which are claimed to keep the combustion chambers cleaner than conventional fuels. This is said, in the long term, to prevent a build-up of deposits which can lessen the efficiency of the engine, and so adversely affect the fuel consumption and performance.

No comment will be made here on the differences between fuels with and without additives. However, their use seems to be spreading to supermarket brands as well, even though certain companies claim that their additives are more effective than others. It is a confusing picture which is continually changing. To sum up, you certainly will not do any long-term harm to your engine by using cheaper fuels, and if you look carefully, you may find that even the cheaper brands contain additives.

Oil

Many British car owners are said to be largely indifferent to the oil they use in their cars, unlike German owners who crave the latest oil technology. The result is that you will find a huge variety of oils available for your car, from astonishingly cheap multi-grades to very expensive synthetic oils.

Before you select your oil, it is worth considering where you buy it. If you check the oil level in your engine when you fill up with fuel, and then buy a litre when you need it, you are almost certainly paying the highest price possible. Oil is very much cheaper if you buy it by the five-litres. If you do this, you can, of course, check and top up your oil level any time you wish.

Choosing the brand of oil is much more difficult. At the top end of the scale are synthetic oils, which can cost over £30 for five litres. This type of oil withstands the worst extremes, continuing to do its job of lubricating and cooling an engine subjected to the harshest driving conditions. Thus it is most likely to be chosen for high-performance cars and those driven very hard. Synthetic oils stay in grade longer, too, which means you can in theory run longer between oil changes because they deteriorate less.

As much as the oil companies would like us all to change to expensive synthetics, the most popular engine oils are the mid-priced multi-grades. These tend to cost in the region of £10 to £15 for 5 litres. Perhaps the most familiar names are Castrol GTX and Duckhams, but every major fuel company offers its own brand which is of an equivalent quality. You are unlikely to go wrong by picking one of these.

At the bottom end of the scale are the budget multi-grade oils which you will find in car accessory shops and supermarkets, even petrol stations, for anything between £4 and £8. Should you buy one of these? If you run an old banger, or your car uses or leaks a lot of oil, they will probably be OK. But it is not really worth cutting corners on a good car where a mid-range oil will probably only set you back another £10 to £15 a year.

There is absolutely no point in adding oil to your engine which is of a higher quality or grade than that already there. If you want to upgrade, then start with an oil change to the type you want, and go from there. Finally, do not skimp on oil changes (and oil filter changes) to save money. It does not pay benefits in the long run.

Tyres

Like engine oils, car tyres vary greatly in price. In a *Which?* test (April 1994) of tyres for family cars, the popular 155 R 13 size ranged from £22 to £49 per tyre, depending upon the make and the sales outlet. It is unfortunately nigh on impossible to judge the qualities of a tyre yourself without first-hand experience. The *Which?* overall Best Buy in this category was the Pirelli P1000, which scored top marks for dry- and wet-road grip, had average tyre life and is easy to find.

In a larger tyre size, 175/70 R 13, the Michelin MXT70 was the Best Buy. Despite its expense, it combined good grip and comfort with a long tyre life. If you want a cheaper tyre with a shorter life, the Fulda Diadem 2, Nokia Rollster TS, Pneumant P47 and Vredestein Sprint + fit the bill and perform well, but are harder to find.

Cheaper still are retread or remould tyres. These are used tyres which have had their outer layers stripped away and replaced with a new tread. They are made to a British Standard and should be marked either BSAU144b or BSAU144e. If you see a retread with neither of these markings, do not buy it, no matter how cheap it is.

One cheaper alternative you should never consider is part-worn (second-hand) tyres. Although they may have enough tread to be legal, there is no way of knowing how they have been used before. They may have been damaged in a way which is not apparent to the non-expert eye.

D-i-y servicing

Carrying out your own service on your car can save a considerable amount of money. Most cars have two levels of routine service, sometimes referred to as the minor and major service, with an additional third type (the major with additional items) perhaps every 36,000 miles.

The minor service is usually very straightforward, and may consist of merely changing the engine oil and oil filter. If you have a set of ramps (you should *never* work under a car which is supported by a jack) and a few spanners, the task could take less than half an hour for a cost of perhaps £15. Although this sounds good value you could well find that there are garages and 'fast-fits' offering the same service for much the same price. With d-i-y, of course, you will still be left with some oil from the five-litre container you purchased for top-ups at a later date, and you can choose your brand of oil.

More involved car servicing is likely to be the preserve of the enthusiastic do-it-yourselfer. Much can be achieved, but with the ever-increasing complexity of modern cars there will be tasks which will be impossible without the equipment found in the specialised workshop.

Alternative spare parts

Car accessory shops and motor factors (shops which deal in just the hardware for cars, rather than cosmetic accessories) have long been in the business of selling spare parts for cars which are cheaper than the originals from the franchised dealer. The car manufacturers tend to argue that these parts do not have to conform to their own rigorous standards. On the other hand, many parts manufacturers claim that they have their own standards which are just as good.

Clearly you need to exercise some form of judgment when buying non-original parts for your car. You need to compare prices carefully, as many official parts have been reduced in price recently in order to attract custom back to the franchised dealers. You may decide that you will continue to buy safety-related spares from the car dealer, and other cheaper parts from the car accessory shop.

Low-cost servicing

Nowadays it is easy to find plenty of independent garages and fast-fit-type outlets which offer to service your car for a fixed price. The advantage of taking your car to one of these places is that you know before you leave the car exactly how much your bill will be, and it will often be less than a main dealer will charge.

You should, however, consider a number of points. In reaction to these fixed-price offers, many franchised dealers will do the same – quote you a fixed priced for a service and, indeed, a number of other routine tasks, such as a clutch replacement. So it is easy to make comparisons over the telephone before you commit yourself.

Second, if you take your car to an authorised dealer for a 'proper' service, you know that it should be done in accordance with the car manufacturer's recommendations for that particular model. That is not likely to be the case at other servicing outlets, where a standard service will have been designed to suit most cars, and is unlikely to deal with the peculiarities of your particular model. We say 'proper' service, because you will find even franchised dealers offering special service deals (spring, summer holiday or winter services are common), which are more limited than the full job.

Third, there is the matter of the service history of the car. As mentioned earlier in the book, you may invalidate any guarantee if you do not have the car serviced by an authorised dealer. You will also find that having a fully stamped services book showing that all the work has been carried out by a franchised dealer will help maximise the resale value when it is time to sell.

Goodwill payments

In the normal course of events, once the warranty on a new car has expired, you will have to pay for any repairs needed from your own pocket. Most car manufacturers and importers, however, are prepared to consider individual claims for repairs outside the warranty period, as long as the car has been rigorously looked after by the owner according to the prescribed service schedule. You will have to pay for the work to be carried out at the time you collect your car from the garage, but ask them to put in for a 'goodwill' payment to the manufacturer. You may then find that the manufacturer will give a sympathetic refund of part of the cost of the repair. A newish car with a full service record at a franchised dealership will be considered most favourably, though some car manufacturers deal with goodwill claims far more sympathetically than others.

GETTING THE MOST FROM YOUR CAR SERVICE

The results of *Which?* investigations into garage servicing produce depressingly similar results. While nearly all carry out a fair job of doing the obvious things, like changing the spark plugs, oil and oil filter, many fall down on other areas of the service. In the October 1993 *Which?* report, the results showed:

- on 36 services carried out, only two were rated as 'good', 19 were 'poor' or 'very poor' and the rest 'average'
- the standard of servicing at Ford, Vauxhall and Rover dealers was no better than at independent garages.

So what can you do to ensure you get the best from your garage? Unfortunately, there is no foolproof way to check that all the work has been done properly – if you are that mechanically competent you will probably do the work yourself anyway. But you can take a series of steps to minimise the risk of difficulties:

- telephone several garages to get quotations for the cost of your service. Make sure that the quote includes the cost of parts, labour and VAT for easy comparison
- franchised dealers should always quote the price based upon the manufacturer's recommended service schedule, but independents may not. If you decide to use an independent, show them the manufacturer's service schedule, which should be in your service handbook, and ask for the service to be based on this
- make a list of specific items or problems you would like checked or repaired. It is also worth asking the garage to return to you any old parts it has replaced
- set a maximum total price for the repairs, or insist that the garage telephones you before it carries out any work on top of that to which you originally agreed. If it says repairs do need carrying out, do not feel pressurised into having them

done there and then. Get an itemised price (for parts, labour and VAT) for every item of work necessary before deciding on whether to sanction it

- after the service, check the invoice to ensure that you have not been charged for things you did not want.

CHAPTER 5

THE MOT TEST

Once your car gets to 3 years of age you must, by law, submit it to an annual MOT test. The idea is that the examination, by an approved garage, will make sure that the car is both safe and keeps exhaust pollution to an acceptable level. The objectives of the test are sound and reasonable, though the fact that annually a third of the cars which are submitted for the test fail means that it is a visit to the garage that few owners undertake with total confidence. That *Which?* investigations have shown that few garages actually do the job properly is also an obvious cause for concern.

WHAT THE MOT TEST INVOLVES

The cost of the MOT test at the time of writing is £23.50, though you may find garages offering to do the job for as little as half that. It can only be carried out by a garage approved by the Vehicle Inspectorate, an Executive Agency in the Department of Transport. Some garages do not go to the trouble and expense of getting approval for MOTs, relying instead on a relationship with a nearby approved workshop to do the job for them.

The test generally takes around half an hour and covers the following points:

1 The **lights** must work correctly and point in the right direction.

2 The **steering** must be in good working order, and properly adjusted.
3 The **wheel bearings** must be adjusted correctly and work efficiently.
4 The **suspension** parts must not be damaged or show signs of excessive wear.
5 Any **suspension subframes** must not be badly corroded or distorted.
6 The **shock absorbers** must not show any signs of leaks or wear.
7 The **handbrake and foot brake** must not only work properly, but there should be no signs of serious deterioration in the mechanisms or pipes under the car.
8 The **wheels** must not be cracked, damaged or distorted.
9 The **tyres** must be within the legal limits.
10 The **wipers, washers** and **horn** must all work correctly.
11 There must be no leaks in the **exhaust** system.
12 The **chassis structure** has to be sound.
13 The **seat-belts** must work properly and be attached to a solid part of the car.
14 The **windscreen** must not be damaged in front of the driver.
15 The **fuel** tank must be sound.
16 The **mirrors, number plates** and **rear fog lamps** will be checked.
17 The exhaust **emissions** will be checked to make sure that they fall within certain limits.

That, very briefly, outlines the areas the MOT tester will be looking at when he goes over your car. There is, not surprisingly, a great deal of detail surrounding each particular point which is outlined in the MOT testers' manual.

WHAT THE MOT DOES NOT GUARANTEE

Through a bizarre twist in the regulations, although an MOT certificate is valid for one year, the Department of Transport says that an MOT refers only to the condition of the car at the time of the test. You might think that if you bought a car with a brand-new MOT only to discover some serious structural rust a week later, you would have some form of comeback. After all, that rust must have been there when the test was carried out, and could only have been overlooked by negligence or criminal intent. Ridiculously, that is not the case. The garage carrying out the MOT cannot be held responsible for *any* fault covered by the test, even if it is discovered five minutes after leaving the testing station.

This fact, and the result of *Which?* investigations into MOT testing, means that you would be foolish to rely upon the MOT test as a seal of approval for your car, or one you are hoping to buy. In 1993, *Which?* put six cars through six MOT tests each, with highly worrying results:

- its experts agreed in full with the verdict of *only one* of the 36 MOT inspections
- testers missed many failure points, including safety-critical items
- many testers also failed items which should have passed
- eight garages passed cars which should have failed.

Changes to the MOT

The government reacted to this *Which?* report by announcing some more changes to the way MOT tests are carried out, to be introduced sometime in the future. There will be three major improvements:

- testers will get more training
- the Vehicle Inspectorate will carry out better checks on MOT stations, and improve its system of applying penalties where mistakes are made
- a review of the possibilities of computerising the MOT testing scheme will be undertaken.

In addition, as an anti-theft measure, you will soon be required to take the car's Vehicle Registration Document with you in order to get an MOT certificate.

PREPARING YOUR CAR FOR THE MOT

As has been pointed out earlier in this chapter, the MOT test is highly involved if it is done correctly. There is no real hope that you, as a private car owner, can duplicate the test at home to make sure that the car really is roadworthy before you take it along for the MOT. But there are some sensible, simple checks that you can easily carry out which could make the difference between a pass and fail and save you the cost of a re-test:

- a common MOT failure point is the lights. Check that they are all working, lenses are not missing, badly cracked, broken or discoloured and that the headlamps do not dazzle. You will need an assistant to sit in the car to press the brake pedal to check the rear brake lights – on many cars these will work only with the ignition switched on
- check that the wiper blades are not worn or damaged – even a tiny split can be a reason for failure. The windscreen washers are also vital – they must point at the right part of the screen and supply a reasonable stream of clean water
- make sure that the horn is working
- a noisy exhaust probably means that there is a hole in it and a replacement of at least part of the system is necessary
- a smoky exhaust could mean that the car will fail the emission test. Checks are made for two pollutants: carbon monoxide and hydrocarbons. All cars registered from August 1975 (P registration onwards) have to be checked on an exhaust analyser, with the emission limits tightened up for cars registered from August 1983 (A registration onwards). Kit cars, amateur-built vehicles and rotary-engined cars are exempt. However, any car (apart from very old ones) can be failed if it is judged to emit dense blue or black smoke for a continuous period of five seconds at idle
- check the tyre pressures, and the tyres themselves, for cuts, bumps and bulges. Tyres with a tread depth of less than 1.6mm over three-quarters of the width of the tread are illegal (and unsafe)

- make sure that there is no free play in the steering. Stand by the driver's door with the window wound down (and the engine running if the car has power steering), move the steering wheel an inch or so in either direction and check that you can see the front wheels moving. If the steering wheel needs to be moved more than this, there is probably wear in the system which needs attention
- check the brakes by bringing the car to a prompt halt on a clear, straight, flat piece of road. The brakes should not pull the car to one side. Do the same with the handbrake – it is unlikely that the car will pull to one side, but the handbrake should slow the car down noticeably. Finally check that the pedal rubbers are not badly worn

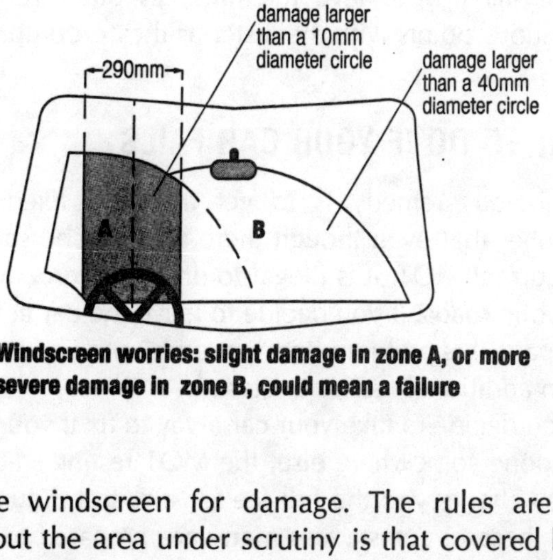

Windscreen worries: slight damage in zone A, or more severe damage in zone B, could mean a failure

- inspect the windscreen for damage. The rules are fairly complex, but the area under scrutiny is that covered by the windscreen wipers. Your car will fail the test if there is any damage in a 290mm vertical strip in front of the driver (zone A in the diagram above) that cannot be contained in a circle of 10mm diameter or less, about half the size of a 5p coin. In the rest of the wiper area (zone B), damage must be containable within a 40mm diameter circle. Your car will also fail if a combination of minor damage seriously restricts your view, or if you have stickers in either zone – unless they are 'official' ones such as the vehicle licence or a parking permit

- check your number plates for damage, dirt or deterioration. They must not be hidden, even partly, by things like a tow-bar. And if you have adjusted the spacing of the letters or disguised them to produce a witty word, your car can be failed.

Carrying out all the above checks should take no more than 20 minutes and will cut down on the chances of your car failing its MOT on the more obvious points. There is, however, little realistic chance of being one hundred per cent sure that it will pass, because so many of the points require a detailed knowledge of cars and specialist equipment.

Finally, MOT stations are obliged to proved a viewing area alongside or overlooking the test bay. It is a good idea to make use of this if you have the time, as often you can discuss contentious points with the tester as they crop up.

What to do if your car fails

The obvious remedy is to get the fault fixed. You should remember that even though there may still be some life left in your current MOT, it is illegal to drive an unroadworthy car on the public roads. If you decide to leave the car at the garage for the repairs this problem does not arise, *and* you will not have to pay an additional fee for a retest.

If you decide to take your car away to fix it yourself or get the work done somewhere else, the MOT testing station has every right to charge you the full fee for a re-test. You may find that under these circumstances many are prepared to offer a lower fee or even do it for no charge at all, though you should check this before you leave.

A contentious point about MOT testing is the worry about phoney repairs. *Which?* found that nearly half the garages it visited failed items which were acceptable in terms of the test. That could be due to incompetence or lack of clarity in the MOT testing manual. But it could also be because the garage is trying to generate extra repair work for itself and finds MOT failures a very useful source of this type of revenue.

If you disagree with the verdict, or some of the failure points, you can appeal, using form VT17. You have to pay the Vehicle Inspectorate for a retest, but if the initial verdict is overturned, you get your money back. Testing stations must keep supplies of VT17s and display a poster explaining the appeal procedure. The Vehicle Inspectorate will arrange to re-inspect your car within a couple of working days.

CHAPTER 6

GETTING INSURED

For most car owners, the cost of insurance will be a major factor in the overall running costs. This and the many changes which have been undertaken in the insurance industry in recent years make it imperative that you understand how your premiums are calculated and regularly review the options in terms of cover and insurer.

HOW YOUR PREMIUM IS WORKED OUT

Like every other form of insurance, the premium for your car policy is based upon the risk of you making a claim. If your particular circumstances indicate that there is a low chance of your insurance company having to deal with a claim over the next year, your premium will be lower than that for a more 'risky' proposition.

Of course, it is not quite that simple. The insurer will also take into account whether any claim is likely to be a costly one. All other things being equal, an accident involving a Mini has a good chance of involving lower repair bills than one involving a Rolls-Royce, so the premiums have to reflect this 'cost of repair' aspect too.

Insurers understand that every driver and his or her car is a unique proposition – in an ideal world it would be possible for each case to considered on its merits before arriving at a carefully calculated premium. In practice this is not really possible, so insurance companies tend to look hard at four major factors: the precise model of car, your age, where you live, and your insurance history.

Your car

Virtually every car on sale in the UK has been allocated a rating on a 20-point scale. At the bottom end is the basic Mini, in Group 1, at the other end, in Group 20, come the Ferraris and Rolls-Royces. Exactly where your car falls in the scale will determine the starting point for your premium calculation.

There are many aspects of a car which are taken into account to arrive at the insurance group, of which performance plays a major part. A two-litre Volkswagen Golf GTi, for example, falls into Group 14, whereas the more mundane Golf 1.4 CL is in Group 6. A Vauxhall Cavalier 1.6 LS is Group 7 compared with Group 12 for the two-litre CDi.

Performance is not everything. It is easy to select a group of cars which have the same new price, and have similar performance, yet vary greatly in insurance cost. This can be perplexing for the owner who is asked to pay premiums he or she considers unreasonable, but there is usually a simple explanation. If the cost of spare parts is higher, the insurance will be more. While some manufacturers take great care to ensure that their cars are cheap and easy to repair after an accident, others place less emphasis on this and consequently their cars are higher-rated.

Security

Security features are a factor too. The car insurance industry has established a set of standards for car security. Each new car is judged on a number of features, like an alarm system or high-security door locks, with the intention that well-protected cars will be cheaper to insure. Unfortunately, this recent development is not quite as encouraging as it sounds from the insurance premium point of view. Even with a whole raft of security features, your premium will not drop by more than one point on the twenty-point scale.

What is more, at the time of writing these security devices

generally need to be supplied with your car as part of its *standard equipment*. Security systems fitted as optional extras rarely make any difference to your premium. The exception are devices which have been approved by the Association of British Insurers, where some insurance companies do offer their customers a discount if they have such a device fitted. Most are expensive immobilisers rather than the cheap type of device sold in car accessory shops, but this may change in the future.

Some cars are so much at risk from theft that you may find it impossible to get cover without the addition of an approved immobiliser. Cars like the Ford Sierra Cosworth have become such targets for thieves that few insurers are interested in providing cover at all, while almost all will require you to take special precautions, such as fitted improved security, before they will issue a policy.

Cars to look out for

With car manufacturers forced to pay more attention to insurance costs, newly introduced models can often be cheaper to insure than the cars they replace. Within each category of car there will always be some that stand out as either conspicuously cheap or expensive for their size and cost.

Bargain basement

A huge variation in insurance rates exists with these cheap cars, largely because the group includes budget models from the major Western manufacturers as well as much bigger cars from eastern Europe.

Cheap Citroën 2CV (Group 1), Fiat 126 (1), Fiat Panda (1), most Minis (1–2)

Expensive Lada Samara 1.5 (6–7), FSO Polonez (8), Yugo Sana (10)

Superminis

There is quite a big variation in premiums here. The cheapest cars to insure are from the big European manufacturers. Any kind of GTi is expensive.

Cheap Fiat Uno 45 (2–3), old Ford Fiesta 950 (2–3), Fiat Punto 55 (3), Peugeot 106 1.0 (3), Renault Clio Campus 1.2 (3), Vauxhall Corsa 1.2 (3)

Expensive Daihatsu Charade (8–11), Mitsubishi Colt (8–12), all GTis

Small family cars

Go for older, simple cars here – despite the design advantages of modern cars, many cost a lot more to insure. The latest Toyota Corolla, for example, is car-for-car three points higher than the model it replaced. Convertibles also add a point or two over the saloon or hatchback.

Cheap Ford Escort 1.3 (4–5), Peugeot 309 1.1 and 1.3 (4–5), Renault 9/11 1.1 and 1.2 (4), Vauxhall Astra 1.2 (5)

Expensive Alfa 33 (10–13), Daihatsu Applause (10), Lancia Delta/Prisma (11–14)

Large family cars

The variation in insurance premium is wide. The average car falls in Groups 10–12. The main factors affecting premiums are the car's manufacturer and the size of the engine, though 'posh' trim levels tend, on the whole, to push up the rating by a group.

Cheap Citroën BX 1.4 (5), Nissan Bluebird 1.6/1.8 (5–6), Peugeot 405 1.6 (6–7), Montego 1.3 (6), Vauxhall Cavalier 1.4 base (5)

Expensive Alfa 75 (15–16), Audi 80 (12–15), BMW 3 Series (12–15), Mitsubishi Galant (12–16), Subaru Legacy (9–17), Volvo 240 (13–15)

People carriers

These specially designed seven- or eight-seater estate cars can be surprisingly expensive to insure.

Cheap Toyota Space Cruiser (10)

Expensive Renault Espace (14–15)

Executive cars

Few of these cars will be cheap to insure. Engine capacity plays a vital part in determining the insurance groupings, and if you can tolerate the rather flat performance of the 1.8 litre versions (mostly only available second-hand now), you will get the lowest insurance bill.

Cheap Ford Granada 1.8 (10), Peugeot 505 1.8 (10), Vauxhall Carlton 1.8 (8–10)

Expensive Alfa 164 (14–17), Honda Legend (15–16), Volvo 940 (from 15)

Luxury cars

All luxury cars will be very expensive to insure. While that may not matter to the person spending £30,000–£40,000 on a brand new car, it will certainly be a major factor in the second-hand market.

Cheap Jaguar saloons with small engines (14–15), Vauxhall Senator 2.5/2.6 (12–13)

Expensive All the rest

Off-roaders

These huge vehicles can be surprisingly economical to insure. No doubt their rugged nature and the fact that the performance of most is pretty mediocre have something to do with it.

Cheap Asia Rocsta (6), Daihatsu Fourtrak (8), Lada Niva (8), Land Rover (5–7), Suzuki SJ and Samurai (6)

Expensive Land Rover Discovery (12–13), Range Rover (13–14), Mercedes G-Wagon (12), Mitsubishi Shogun (12–15), Toyota Land Cruiser (12)

Your age

Age and driving experience are hugely important in arriving at the premium. Once you have reached 25 years old you can get cover at 'normal' rates for the majority of cars. Below this age you may well find that the insurer will 'load' the premium by adding anything from 15 per cent to 100 per cent, depending upon your precise age and experience. You will probably also have a higher compulsory accidental damage excess.

Getting insurance for young drivers has become particularly expensive, as mounting evidence points to the greatly increased risk of an accident – and a claim – in the first years of driving for the under-21s.

Middle-age is viewed much more favourably, with the best deals on premiums available by shopping around. Insurers like to have mature, steady drivers with ordinary cars on their books, and some will concentrate on these owners to the exclusion of others, which can result in some very attractive premiums.

Elderly drivers may find that the cost of insurance starts to rise again, particularly if they have an accident. This is a reflection of the view of certain insurers that the very old are not as alert and responsive as they once were.

Where you live

Drivers in densely populated areas suffer a double problem: on the roads there is a greater chance of an accident than in the quieter countryside, and the incidence of theft and break-ins is much higher. Just like they have done with cars, insurers have developed a ranking system for different areas of the UK, which can make a big difference to your premium. The lowest-rated areas for car insurance are counties like Cornwall, Suffolk and Dyfed. The highest are the inner-city areas of London, Liverpool and Glasgow. If you keep your car in a garage, particularly in a highly rated area, you may well find that you get a more favourable rate. In some high-rate areas, you may have to have a garage to get a quote.

Your insurance history

A good insurance record can go a long way towards reducing your premiums. No-claims discount (also known as no-claims bonus) is awarded for each year you drive without making a claim. Exactly how much the no-claims discount reduces your premium varies from company to company, but typically after one year's claim-free motoring you will be entitled to a 30 per cent discount, then 40, 50 and 60 per cent after four years. The maximum figure used by many insurers is 60 per cent but a few extend it to 65 per cent after five years.

No-claims discount is transferable from company to company, so, if you have 'earned', say, a 40 per cent reduction after two years motoring and your company then seems a little expensive, other insurers will give you the same level of discount on their policy, up to their normal maximum.

On the other hand, if you have had recent accidents you may find that you are doubly penalised. Not only may you have lost your no-claims discount, you may well find that insurers load your basic premium because you are now considered to be a bad risk. Similarly, prosecutions for motoring offences can result also in a premium loading, which will vary according to the seriousness of the offence. While a single speeding conviction will probably not affect your premium at all, a drink-drive offence will be viewed most unfavourably and could result in higher premiums for up to 10 years.

Other factors

Drivers in certain occupations are said to have a higher or lower risk of an accident. Some insurers look more favourably on policyholders who are teachers, civil servants or bank officers, for example, while most charger higher premiums for publicans, musicians, journalists and professional sportsmen and women.

If you use your car for **business** the premium may be higher, depending on exactly what you do. The standard Class 1 insurance covers social domestic and pleasure use, and may allow limited business use. Class 2, perhaps 25 to 30 per cent more expensive, gives cover for most business use. Class 3 is for commercial travellers and cars used by the motor trade, with premiums which tend to be 25 to 30 per cent higher still.

CUTTING THE COSTS

Almost every insurer will be able to offer you opportunities to reduce your bill further by accepting some restrictions on your policy.

Limit the drivers

Insurance policies can cover the car no matter who is driving it (above a certain age). But you could save as much as 20 per cent by naming yourself as the only driver, or 10 per cent by restricting cover to yourself and your spouse.

Pay the first part of the claim

Comprehensive policies, which cover accident damage to your car as well as to other people and their property, often require you to accept an 'excess' of £50 to £100. This is the amount you have to pay from your own pocket each time you claim. If, however, you are prepared to accept an additional ('voluntary') excess, perhaps another £100 to £250, you will find that the premiums come down.

Business use

You should check whether your policy automatically covers you for business use. If you do not need it, and are prepared to limit the use of the car to social, domestic and pleasure purposes, some companies will give an additional discount.

Introductory discounts

These are often available to drivers over 23 who are insuring for the first time. You would, however, need to have had some experience after passing your test, with most insurers looking for a full licence held for at least 12 months.

Garaging

One way to get round the problems of theft and damage to your car in inner-city areas is to keep it garaged overnight. Insurance companies recognise this as an added safeguard and may offer a reduction on your premium.

Level of cover

Finally, there is the important consideration of the level of cover you have. **Comprehensive** insurance deals with almost any eventuality, from damage to other people, their cars and property, to covering the cost of repairs to your own car. The major alternative, aimed at older, low-value cars, is **third party, fire and theft** cover, which as well as covering the risks of fire and theft to your car, covers your legal requirements to other people. What it does not do is pay for your own repairs, but as long as your car is not worth a great deal you may consider the lower premiums offset the risk.

You can buy even lower levels of insurance cover. **Third party** is the legal minimum, which covers you and your passengers for personal liability for injury to anyone or damage to you or your passengers' property. Damage to your own car is not covered. Very few insurers are prepared to offer this minimal cover.

Preserving your no-claims discount

As the no-claims discount takes so many years to accumulate, and makes such a big difference to your final bill for car insurance, it is worth considering very carefully any situation which might affect it. The first important factor here is that the no-claims discount relates to a claim, not a fault. Simply, if you make a claim on your car insurance policy, your no-claims discount is likely to be affected – it does not matter whose fault the accident was. Many drivers consider it unfair when confronted with a situation where bonus is lost through no fault of their own. Insurers can argue, however, that if the accident was entirely another party's fault, you could have claimed directly from them.

There are ways around this problem, however. One is additional legal cost insurance. This is a relatively recent concept which many insurers and brokers offer to their clients for a small fee – typically £5 to £10 per annum. If you do have to claim off your own policy, this legal expenses insurance can be invoked to pursue the costs of the accident against the guilty party. If these costs are recovered, the cost of your car repairs will go directly to your insurer, you will get a cheque for the 'excess' you had to pay, and your no-claims bonus will be reinstated.

Another option is the protected no-claims discount. Once you have earned the maximum allowance, normally a 60 per cent discount, you can ask for that discount to be protected at that level so that it is not reduced after a claim. There will always be limitations, such as being allowed to make just two claims in any five-year period, after which the protection is removed. The restrictions vary from company to company, as does the cost. Sometimes protected no-claims bonus is automatically included in the standard policy, with other insurers you may have to pay as much as 20 per cent on top of the price of the standard policy.

No matter what type of policy, it is unlikely that you will lose all of your bonus after one claim. The standard procedure is to reduce your discount by the equivalent of two years, so that 60 per cent would drop to 40 at the next renewal time, 50 per cent to 30, and 40 per cent to nil.

After a serious accident your car may be so badly damaged that it is deemed by the insurer to be a 'write off'. That means the insurer judges the cost of repair to be uneconomic, usually because the cost is going to be higher than the value of the car. How much you will then get paid will depend to an extent on the small print. It may be the value of the car before the accident, or it may be the cost of replacing your car with something similar. If your car is less than six months or a year old, many policies provide for a brand-new replacement.

Almost certainly you will find that your policy is cancelled (with no refund of premium for the period left to run) because the car you insured no longer exists. You will therefore need to take out a new policy when you buy a replacement car.

HOW TO BUY CAR INSURANCE

Brokers

Brokers deal in insurance from both the major household name insurance companies and the Lloyd's syndicates. Both will provide reliable cover for your car, though quite which type will provide the most favourable quotation will depend upon your particular circumstances.

The advantage of dealing with brokers is that a large number of insurers will be on their books and they will be able to use their experience to home in on those likely to offer you the best deal. When your premium comes up for renewal each year, a good broker will look again at your requirements to see if it can come up with a better quotation.

So far so good, but as together there are hundreds of companies and Lloyd's syndicates selling insurance in the UK, even the largest broker can only hope to offer a representative selection. You will therefore find that some brokers specialise in certain types of insurance – young drivers, those with convictions, sports cars and so on – so should know their area of the market rather better than a more general broker. You can get an idea of who specialises in what by looking in your local *Yellow Pages* or *Thompson* directory. Some brokers operate from a single local office, others are part of nationwide chains, like the AA, Hill House Hammond, Swinton and the RAC.

Direct sell

Buying insurance over the telephone has become the big growth area in the 1990s. Direct sellers are usually part of a major insurance group. They claim to be cheaper because they do not pay commission to brokers and agents, but they are often choosy about who they are prepared to insure – 'bad' risks are often discouraged. You will find many advertising in your local business telephone directory.

Classic car insurance

If you own an old car which could be considered a 'classic' you could find some particularly good insurance deals. To qualify, you usually need to belong to the car club associated with your model – the MG Car Club or Jaguar Drivers Club, for example. The membership fee is rarely more than £25 a year, for which you can expect a newsletter with details of specialist insurers.

You will have to get your car valued by a club official, and your premium will then be based upon this 'agreed value', which is the sum which will be paid out without question if your car is stolen or written off. There are usually some serious restrictions on your annual mileage – as few as 3,000 on some polices – but this can usually be increased for an additional charge.

The great advantage of classic car insurance is that you can arrange comprehensive cover very cheaply, even if you do not have any no-claims discount, and some companies do not differentiate much between ordinary and sports cars. Classic car magazines are a good starting pcint for tracking down the right car club and finding lists of specialist brokers.

CHAPTER 7

Car Security

Car crime has become one of the big growth areas of the 1990s, accounting for over a quarter of all recorded crime in the UK. The statistics make grim reading: one car is stolen every minute; a theft from a car happens every 35 seconds; in a year, 1 in 25 cars has something stolen from it; and 1 in 40 is actually stolen. A report published by the RAC in May 1994 put England and Wales at the top of the international car-crime league, even above the USA.

Cars are stolen for three main purposes. By far the most significant, accounting for around two-thirds of thefts, is for one-off use. This includes 'joy-riding', stealing a car to use in another crime or simply taking a car to get home after the last bus has left. Many of these stolen vehicles are dumped a few hours later.

Around a quarter of cars are stolen by 'professional' thieves. The cars either go through an identity change (known as 'ringing') before being sold on, or are stripped down for the spare parts. Finally, a proportion of cars which have been reported as stolen, are, in fact, being used by the owners as attempts to defraud their insurance companies. This is more common with older cars which have become less economic to repair for the MOT or after an accident.

Security improvements in new cars

Over the years the security of newly designed cars has gradually been improved. Unfortunately, the thief has, by and large, managed to discover ways around most forms of new protection. This is particularly true of steering column locks, which were hailed as a great step forward when introduced, but quickly became just another hindrance which was simple to overcome. Since 1992, however, many new models have been fitted with security features which may prove far more effective. The key features you should look for in a new car are given below.

Central door locking

This has one major advantage: as long as you remember to lock the driver's door the rest of the car will be locked too. This may sound obvious, but drivers still forget to lock their cars fully when leaving them.

Deadlocks

A deadlock has the normal key-operated locking position, plus an additional high security one. Ordinary door locks can sometimes be overcome by tampering with the mechanism inside the door – it is no secret that thieves enter cars by poking a tool between the window and door frame and fiddling around until the lock releases. A deadlocked car generally resists such attacks much better than a traditional lock. More importantly, you cannot open a deadlocked car from inside, so the casual thief who smashes a window to reach the locks inside will not be able to open a door (though he may still be able to reach the radio).

There have been some worries that young children who may have been locked into a car by their parents to keep them safe while shopping could then not be released in an emergency. For this reason, many car manufacturers force you to operate the deadlock positively by making an extra turn of the key – otherwise only the standard locks will be in operation. While this has its advantages, it does mean that for your car to be fully secure at all times, you must make sure you deadlock it properly before leaving it. Some cars allow you to do this by remote control.

Alarms

Car alarms fall into two categories – those approved by the car manufacturer itself, and those sold as accessories for any make of car; the accessory side is covered later in this chapter.

It has become increasingly common for car manufacturers to incorporate an alarm into the original design of the car. That is a good idea, because all the complicated electrical wiring can be hidden away as the car is built, increasing both security and reliability. A built-in alarm is also a favoured option because every car manufacturer will try to make sure that the alarm works well: it is not in their interests to have an alarm system which is prone to going off at the wrong time. So you can reckon that any factory-fitted car alarm should offer a reasonable level of protection, even if it is not the latest thing in terms of sophistication and features. Many car manufacturers, however, particularly importers from the Far East, rely upon their dealers to fit the alarm. In theory, you should also get a good job if you take this route, though you need to check that the dealer really does fit an alarm system approved by the importer, rather than one he can buy more cheaply elsewhere. There is nothing wrong with accessory alarms from independent sources, but you should be feel more reassured if you know the alarm has been tried out before in your particular model of car.

Electronic immobilisers

This is a more recent innovation than the car alarm. An immobiliser is installed into a car's wiring system so that it is (in theory) impossible to start the engine without the correct device. Usually this is a small additional key with a coded micro-chip – you insert the key into a socket in the dashboard each time you want to start the engine. On certain cars there is a key pad, where you have to key in a secret number to override the immobiliser. Or it may be operated by remote control.

The virtue of the immobiliser over the standard ignition cut-out which is incorporated into many alarm systems is that it is much more difficult to overcome. The wiring is usually designed to be extremely confusing for a potential thief, so that even if the wires are cut and re-routed, the chances of getting the engine going are very small.

At the moment only a few manufacturers fit immobilisers to their cars as standard, but the number is likely to increase. Ford has introduced a very clever system where the electronic chip is built into the ignition key, so that each time you insert the key the immobiliser is de-activated. There are several companies on the market fitting immobilisers as optional extras.

Vehicle identification

Every car has its own vehicle identification number (VIN) which is displayed in the engine compartment. A recent security development is 'visible VIN', where a plate is securely bonded into an inaccessible but visible position (usually under the base of the windscreen). The idea is that if the car is stolen and 'ringed', it is extremely difficult to change all the identifying tags throughout the car, so a potential buyer merely has to make sure that VIN numbers are all the same.

A clever development of this is to print the VIN on a large number of micro dots, about the size of a pin head. These are then scattered throughout the car during manufacture. If a car is thought to be stolen, these can be located with an special detector and checked to see that all the numbers correlate. Obviously this is far from foolproof, but it does require an enormous amount of tedious work on behalf of the thieves to overcome. This development is confined to luxury cars, where it may be offered as an option.

Secure stereo systems

The car stereo remains an attraction for many opportunist thieves, despite the fact that it is difficult to comprehend why there should still be a strong market for stolen stereos. With some form of radio cassette fitted to nearly every car sold in the UK, the car manufacturers and radio suppliers have developed three main ways to combat stereo theft: security coding, the removable stereo system and the 'unique' stereo.

Security coding has been available for some time. A radio with this feature will not work if the power is cut from it – when it is removed from the car – without the correct code being punched back in. To prevent a thief merely going through all the available numbers until he or she arrives at the correct code, the security system will often let you have only half a dozen tries to get it right before refusing to accept any more attempts for several hours. Although a sound idea in principle, it seems that there are ways of getting round the coding by those with the right electronic equipment.

A more secure alternative is the **removable stereo system**. The set has a small handle built in allowing the complete unit to be slid from the dashboard and taken with you or secreted elsewhere in the car. Unfortunately, most radios are too heavy to carry around comfortably, so drivers, when they do remember to remove them, tuck them under the front seat or in the boot. Thieves know this and may chance a break-in even when there is obviously a hole in the dashboard where the stereo should be.

A more satisfactory alternative is the **removable front panel**. The idea is the same, but with these you merely unclip a portion of the front of the stereo about the size of a small comb, and slip it into your pocket. Replacements for these are so expensive that it is not worth the trouble of stealing the rest of the unit.

Finally, there is the **unique stereo**. This has to be designed into the car from the outset, and its unique layout, often with the controls quite separate from the display, means that it will not fit any other model of car. This is a very strong deterrent as there is absolutely no point in stealing a stereo which can only be fitted into the same model of car, which almost certainly has the same system already.

ADDING SECURITY TO YOUR CAR

There are literally hundreds of devices available to protect your car, from sophisticated items costing £500 which have to be installed by a specialist, to simple locks which can be bought for under £20. Quite which you choose will depend not only upon the depth of your pocket but also the risk you feel your car runs of being attacked or stolen.

Alarms

The cost of car alarms varies enormously – you can buy products under this general description for £30 or £500. So what can you expect, and which features are the important ones to go for?

The dominant feature of every alarm is that it makes a loud noise. At the very cheapest end of the market, this noise might be the sort which is unpleasant for the thief rather than attracting others' attention. There are very easy-to-fit devices with built-in batteries which lock over the steering wheel or fix to the dashboard. When the car is entered, a change in air pressure will set off the internal siren, which is supposed to make it unbearable for the thief to drive away. When *Which?* tested two of these devices in November 1992 it found they were easy to detach and throw out by the determined thief.

More serious alarms are wired into the car's electrical system and will sound a siren under the bonnet to deter the intruder. They range from the simple units operated by a hidden switch inside the car which sound the alarm perhaps 10 seconds after a door has been opened, to devices which detect movement inside the car and are switched on and off by remote control.

When selecting an alarm for your car you should first consider whether you are going to fit it yourself (in which case you will probably be looking for a relatively simple system) or get the job done professionally. Then make up your mind about which of the following features you feel are necessary. By and large the more you have, the higher the level of security.

Engine immobilisation is an important ingredient, preventing the engine from being started when the alarm is in operation.

A **back-up battery** means that even if the thief disconnects or cuts wiring to the car battery, the alarm will still operate – indeed it will probably go off as soon as the car battery is taken out of the electrical circuit.

A car alarm which is operated by **remote control** is more secure than the type with a hidden switch. Check the number of remotes you get if there is more than one driver. Many will also operate the car's central locking at the same time, so check whether this feature is available – it is not universal. Some remote control systems automatically change their code each time they are operated in order to impede 'grabbers'. These devices are used by thieves to pick up the signal from your remote control as you operate it, which they then copy electronically into their own remote.

An alarm may have several different types of sensor built into it, or come with just one with others offered as optional extras. A **direct contact sensor** works in the same way as the switches which control the interior light in the door. **Voltage drop sensors** sense when any electric equipment, such as the starter motor, is switched on. They can be a problem in cars where the cooling fan on the engine runs after the engine has been switched off. **Current sensors** work in a similar way but monitor only the current drawn by certain circuits.

All of these rely upon a change in the car's electrical system being detected. **Ultrasonic detectors**, on the other hand, sense changes in air pressure within the car caused by movement. This is a good principle, but is the main cause of so many alarms sounding unnecessarily on a windy day, when air gets though the vents into the car and causes a disturbance. The trick is to shut these vents (and the windows and sunroof) when you leave the car. Some sensors can be switched off, which is a good idea if, for example, you have a convertible with ultrasonic detectors which you may wish to leave for a short while with the roof down.

Shock sensors detect a sudden movement of the car – if it is bumped, for example. A **tilt sensor** will sound if the car is lifted up to be towed away, or jacked up to remove the wheels.

A **panic mode** on the alarm will allow you to set off the alarm from inside the car in an emergency, or possibly from outside if you see someone trying to break in. Some alarms will **report back**, which means you will get an indication that the alarm had gone off while you were away from the car.

Finally, make sure the alarm offers a good visual deterrent to any potential criminal. After all, it is better for the thief to be deterred *before* attempting to break in rather than after, when the alarm sounds.

Electronic immobilisers

The immobilisers described earlier can be fitted to almost any make of car. Most have more than one way of preventing a car from being started, and a thief has to overcome all of them. They are expensive, rarely under £100 in d-i-y form, with the better, professionally fitted devices costing as much as £300 to £400. They do not, of course, prevent a determined thief loading your car on a trailer and taking it away to deal with the immobiliser elsewhere. Nor do they usually include any form of alarm.

Clamps and locks

A vast range of clamps exists, which provides a mechanical and visual deterrent to stealing a car. The two most popular are the **steering wheel to pedal lock** (£10 to £25) and the **steering wheel clamp** (£15 to £40). The former locks the wheel to the clutch or brake pedal. The latter comprises a large steel bar locked to the steering wheel which obstructs movement.

You can also buy **wheel clamps** (£35 to £130), superficially like those used to clamp your car for a parking offence, a **gearlever lock** and **gear-to-handbrake lock**. When *Which?* tested a wide range of mechanical clamps and locks in November 1992 it overcame almost all of them by force or with a few simple tools. Only three scored an acceptable rating for security, and most were poor or worse. Their main value is as a visual deterrent.

Locking wheel nuts

Expensive alloy wheels are an easy target, but can easily be protected with locking wheel nuts. These usually come in sets of four – one locking nut for each wheel – and are easy to fit and use. You *must* remember to keep the key with you in case you have a puncture.

Window etching

Getting all the separate pieces of glass in your car windows etched with the car's registration number is a cheap and easy way to deter the more serious thief. For £5 to £10 (and for nothing with some insurance companies) each piece of glass is indelibly marked with the registration number. To disguise a stolen car for sale a thief then has to replace the glass as well, a costly and time-consuming business.

Tracker

A new car theft measure is the Tracker system, sold through the Automobile Association (see Addresses). A radio device is hidden in one of 30 places within a car. When the car is reported stolen, the device is activated by remote control, and it then transmits a signal which can be picked up by the police, who then attempt to recover your car. A number of patrol cars in most areas of the country are fitted with Tracker detectors and there are others at various points around the M25 as well as at ports around the UK. Tracker can also be used in caravans, 2,000 of which are stolen each year. The cost is relatively high. In 1994, for a car, there is a choice between a one-off lifetime payment of £350 or a first payment of £160, then £61.10 a year subscription. Caravans need a high-powered rechargeable battery and are consequently more expensive – £540 or £295 and £61.10 a year.

APPROVED CAR SECURITY DEVICES

With such a wide variety of products available, and such difficulty in making the correct judgment on effectiveness, the Association of British Insurers has developed an approval scheme for car security devices. At the moment this is restricted to alarms and electronic immobilisers, and it assumes that these have been professionally fitted.

The scheme is in its early days, and only a limited number of products has so far been tested and approved. But this number is likely to increase in the near future. Some car insurers will allow you a discount on your premium if you have an approved security device. To find out the latest details, send a large stamped addressed envelope to Department VS, 51 Gresham Street, London EC2V 7HQ. A list of those devices approved as we went to press is included in Appendix 2.

SENSIBLE PRECAUTIONS

- Always lock your car and set any security devices every time you leave it. The most common area left unlocked is the boot or rear hatch, the second most common, the front passenger door.
- Do not leave anything of value on view. Around 60 per cent of theft from cars is opportunistic, so do not make your car more attractive or tempting to a thief.
- Park in well-lit, busy areas.
- Fit secure audio equipment with security features, preferably including a removable front panel.
- Fit locking wheel nuts, especially to alloy wheels, although normal steel wheels and tyres are stolen too.
- Have all glass marked with the registration number. Thieves are less likely to steal a car for 'ringing' if they have to replace the marked glass.
- Never leave any documents in the car. And anything with your name and address on it makes it easier for a thief to get duplicate documents.
- Consider buying an extra security device. Make sure it is as visible as possible to act as a deterrent to would-be thieves.

CHAPTER 8

Choosing a Safe Car

Everyone wants to be safe in their car. But, until recently, car safety was not really a hot subject and seemed to be ignored by all but Volvo. But was it? While Volvo has certainly produced cars which are safer than the average, and capitalised on that aspect in its advertising, all car manufacturers have to meet certain minimum standards, and many have gone a long way past them. So how do you make sure you are buying the safest car for you and your family?

Which Type of Safety?

You can look at car safety in two different ways:

- how good the car will be at keeping you out of an accident in the first place – primary safety
- how well it will protect you if you do crash – secondary safety.

These are two very different aspects of safety, and a car which is good at one is not necessarily the best at the other. Over the years there have been many developments which should have reduced your risk of being involved in an accident. Wide, radial-ply tyres have vast reserves of grip. Front-wheel-drive has made the handling of everyday cars more predictable. Anti-lock brakes prevent the car from skidding under braking. The list goes on. The trouble is, there is little evidence that these impressive developments have cut down on the *number* of accidents. Some drivers, it seems, merely drive faster to take advantage of the improvements in design and, worse still, have accidents at a higher speed than they may have done in a more mundane car.

THE *WHICH?* CAR SAFETY RATINGS

While it is certainly worth buying a car packed with as many primary safety characteristics as you can afford, it is likely to be more beneficial to aim for one packed with secondary safety features. *Which?* has been testing cars for safety since the early '80s and has now compiled data on over 250 popular models. The rating system is the only one in the world which gives information on the performance of a new car in the whole mix of accidents that it is likely to encounter on the road. A team of highly experienced accident investigators partially strips down a car to examine 50 critical areas – the steering wheel or side structure of the car, for example – which can kill or injure you in an accident. The design of each area is assessed against what is known about how the area kills or injures people, and the best design practice to avoid death and injury. Each area is awarded a numerical score that reflects how well it has been designed and how often that area is likely to be involved in different types of crashes. Good design, therefore, in an area which often causes death or serious injury scores highly, whereas good design in a less important areas adds less to the final score. The numerical scores for each area are added together and then adjusted to take account of the weight of the vehicle because you are likely to be better off in a heavier car.

In Appendix 3 we give a listing of the safety ratings of all the cars *Which?* has tested up to August 1994. Much more attention is paid to designing-in safety into new cars, and you will see the fruit of those efforts in the latest models.

KEY SECONDARY SAFETY FEATURES TO LOOK FOR

While there are many aspects of a car's design on which you cannot make a judgement – the stiffness of the body plays an important part in an accident, for example – you can at least make sure that a car which has not been rated by *Which?* for safety contains some elementary features which will reduce the risk of injury to you or other occupants. Below are outlined a number of factors which should form an important part of your buying decision.

Weight

The weight of a car has a straightforward effect on your safety – generally, the heavier the car, the less likely you are to be injured. The best superminis are only as safe as the average small family car, for example.

Steering wheel

With seat-belt wearing now compulsory for all front-seat occupants, the overall risk of serious injury has been reduced. Another problem, however, has arisen. In a frontal accident there is a real risk that the driver's head will hit the steering wheel causing facial injuries, sometimes serious. An airbag fitted into the centre of the steering wheel addresses this problem. In an accident, the airbag inflates almost instantaneously to cushion your face from the hard parts of the steering wheel. This feature is reckoned to be very worthwhile, though the case for front passenger-side airbags is less clear-cut, and these are not safe if a rearward-facing child restraint is fitted to the front seat.

Air bags are a very recent development in Europe, and you are unlikely to find a car built before 1993 with one. On other cars you should therefore look for a steering wheel hub and spokes that are covered with deep energy-absorbing material, free from hard spots. Bad steering wheels have metallic parts exposed, and/or the bolt in the centre (holding the wheel to the column) close to the surface of the wheel. A thin covering over a prominent bolt will do little to protect you in an accident.

Front seat-belts

Unless it is very old indeed, any car you buy new or used will have inertia-reel front seat-belts. These allow you to move around in normal circumstances, but lock in place in a crash. In principle, they are not as safe as the 'static' belts, which hold you firmly all the time, but inertia reel seat-belts have been accepted as the standard as they are more comfortable, adjust automatically to more or less the right position and, above all, are convenient – so are more likely to be used. If you have trouble getting comfortable wearing a belt you may find one of the many cars with adjustable upper mountings in the doors most suitable.

Two recent developments on seat-belts worth looking out for are **pre-tensioners** and **web locking**. A pre-tensioner is a device, usually attached to the buckle, which yanks the belt back or down at the time of the accident. This tightens it a little more and cuts down on your forward movement. A web lock grasps the belt at the door end to prevent more belt being pulled through the spooled-up webbing. It is difficult to spot either of these yourself on a car, but it is easy enough to check with a car dealer or the manufacturer/importer.

Rear seat-belts

While rear seat-belts have been fitted to new cars by law for some time, and it is now compulsory for rear-seat passengers to wear them, there are still many cars without rear belts. The importance of having them cannot be over-emphasised – not only does an unrestrained rear passenger run the risk of serious injury in an accident, it is also bad news for those in the front seats, who can be severely injured by a rear passenger flying forward.

Even if a car does not have a full set of seat-belts, they are easy enough to install on most cars under 20 years old. Most have the mounting points already built in under the seat cushion and in the rear pillar. The belts themselves range in price from a simple lap belt at around £15 to a full inertia reel unit at double that.

Head restraints

In order to protect your neck in a rear impact, a head restraint needs to be strong, stable and high enough to support your whole head. You should check this out on a car you are considering because there are still many cars around which do not provide enough adjustment for tall people. Remember, too, that those in the back seat are equally in need of protection, though finding cars with rear head restraints is not so easy.

Padding

The purpose of interior padding is to stop your head or other parts of your body hitting hard parts of metalwork. It is very difficult to judge the quality of padding, so the best you can do is to make sure that the car you are considering does not have any exposed parts of metal, especially bolts and hard fittings.

Other matters

There are many other aspects to secondary safety which are impossible for the lay person to judge. *Which?* appraisals are carried out by a team with many years of experience in investigating the causes of injuries in road accidents. Particular areas of concern are:

- the strength of the seat
- hard objects below the dashboard which could injure the driver's and front passenger's legs
- door design, particularly side impact beams and strong door catches
- bodyshell strength
- well-protected fuel system and electrics, to avoid the risk of fire.

There is still a way to go, however, before even the most modern cars incorporate the whole range of possible safety features.

LEARNING TO DRIVE MORE SAFELY

The vast majority of people who pass their driving test take no further tuition, which means that they definitely have no tutored experience on motorways, and may well never have driven on dual carriageways, at night or in the rain.

There is much to be said for some additional guidance in your driving, and it does not necessarily take much additional time or expense. Other than improving your driving standards, an additional safe-driving qualification can help reduce your insurance premiums.

Post-test training

At the time of writing, the Government was proposing a new training scheme for drivers who have recently passed their test. The scheme has been devised by the Driving Standards Agency to improve skills in observation, hazard perception and awareness – factors which are known to make drivers safer but which can take years to acquire on the road. The scheme looks likely to go ahead and would involve six lessons with an approved instructor, covering:

- town driving
- adverse weather conditions
- out of town and rural road driving
- night driving
- dual carriageways
- motorways.

If the scheme has yet to get into motion, the Driving Instructors Association (DIA) offer something very similar. Around a third of all approved driving instructors are members of the DIA, and any can offer a course of lessons after the test has been passed, which covers the same ground as the Driving Standards Agency proposals. Once you have completed the course to a satisfactory standard you will be eligible for an insurance discount through a specialist broker.

Advanced driving

The Institute of Advanced Motorists (IAM) and the Royal Society for the Prevention of Accidents (RoSPA) both promote safer driving by offering 'advanced driving tests'. You can get help and guidance from them about improving your driving standards as well as how to go about dealing with the test itself. Both organisations are able to recommend insurance companies which offer preferential rates to those who have passed the test. Contact IAM on 081-994 4403 and RoSPA on 021-706 8121.

Carrying Children in Cars

Just as it is vital for adults to use seat-belts in cars, it is essential that children are strapped in too. Every year over 9,000 children under 11 years of age are killed or injured in car accidents. The big fear is that a child will be thrown right out of a car, which is easier than you might think, and usually with serious consequences.

It is impossible to support a child properly in your own arms, even if you are securely belted-in yourself. A child's effective weight can increase 20-fold, tearing it free. It is equally dangerous to put one belt around both you and a child. Your weight could well crush the child. The only effective answer is to put a child into a proper child safety restraint every time. The law lays down the following rules:

Children under three In the front seat a child restraint must *always* be worn. In the back seat a child restraint must be used if one is available. If one is not, then the law says that a restraint need not be used.

Children from 3 to 11 As long as the child is under 1.5 metres tall, he or she *must* wear an appropriate child restraint if one is available. If not, then the child *must* wear an adult belt, even though this is not nearly as effective as a proper child seat.

Children 12 and above Older children, and those over 1.5 metres tall, *must* wear an adult belt if one is fitted, wherever they sit in the car.

Choosing a child restraint

All child safety restraints have to undergo a series of approval tests before they can be sold as such. Most manufacturers make their seats to the European Regulation ECE44 as this allows them to be sold throughout Europe. Seats made to these regulations will have a label marked with 'E' followed by a number, referring to the country where the seat was tested. You will probably see mention of ECE44 on the packaging too.

In addition, there are three British Standards for child restraints:

- BS AU 202a for rearward-facing seats
- BS3254 Part 2 for forward-facing seats and booster cushions
- BS AU 185 for booster cushions.

Seats and restraints to any of these standards are suitable for your child. The key factor in selecting the right type of seat is the child's weight, rather than its age.

Stage 1

Weight limit 0 to 10kg

Age range 0 to around 9 months

Price typically £25 to £50

This is a rearward-facing baby seat which can be carried in the front or the back seat of the car – the back is preferable for the child's safety. These seats have built-in straps to hold the child in place.

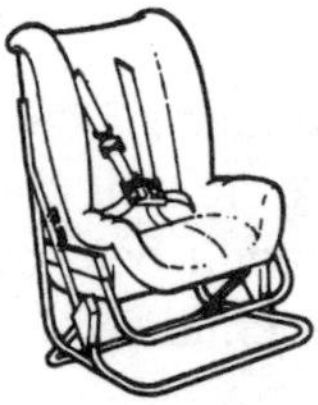

Stage 1–2

Weight limit 0 to 18kg

Age range 0 to around 4 years

Price typically £40 to £80

This can be used as a rearward-facing baby seat until the child is old enough to sit up, and then converted into a forward-facing seat until the child is around four years old. Built-in straps hold the child in place.

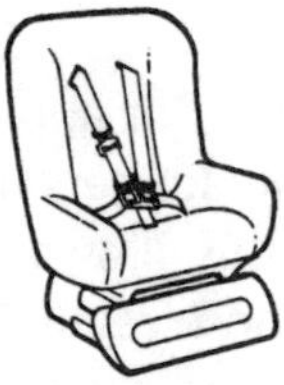

Stage 2

Weight limit 9 to 18kg

Age range around 6 months to 4 years

Price typically £35 to £90

This is a forward-facing seat for children who can sit up. Built-in straps hold the child in place.

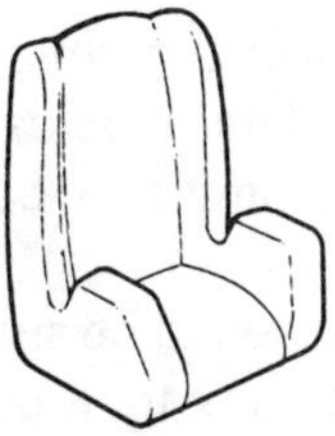

Stage 2–3
Weight limit 9 to 25kg
Age range around 6 months to 6 years
Price typically £50

Seats with a bigger age and weight range than Stage 2 seats, which make use of the adult belts rather than having built-in straps.

Stage 3
Weight limit 15 to 36kg
Age range around 4 months to 11 years
Price typically £10 to £15

These are booster cushions, which raise the child off the car seat so that the adult safety belt fits them properly.

It is immediately obvious from the above list of types of child seat that there is a good deal of overlap in age and weight. You have to decide whether you choose seats which cover a broad age range or those designed for a more particular size of child. *Which?* has tested all types for safety, and while there is every reason to believe that any child seat will provide a great deal of protection in an accident, some are better than others.

For the youngest children, buy a Stage 1 seat rather than a Stage 1–2. The former is generally safer and makes it easier to carry a sleeping baby around. Then move straight to a Stage 2–3 seat, where both the seat and the child are held in place with the adult belt. The trouble with Stage 2 seats, which are held in place with the adult belt and then the child is strapped into a separate harness within the seat, is that with inertia-reel seat-belts the seats move forward too much in an accident. Amazingly, European Regulation ECE44 still allows testing with obsolete static safety belts, which can fasten the seat much tighter. Stage 2–3 seats proved safer in *Which?* tests (August 1993) with the inertia-reel belts.

After that you may still need to buy a booster cushion (Stage 3) to improve the fit of an adult belt around your child. The diagonal section of the seat-belt should pass over the child's shoulder mid-way between the neck and the tip of the shoulder. The lap section should not ride up over the soft tummy area, but sit low on the thighs.

Whatever type of seat you decide to buy, you need to be sure that it is suitable for your particular car. If you cannot try it out before you buy, check that the shop will take it back if it proves to be unsuitable. When you put it in the car, check out the following:

- the car's seat-belt is long enough – most likely to be a problem with rearward-facing or two-way seats
- the car's seat-belt buckle does not rest on the frame of the seat or interfere with it in any way
- the seat-belt holds the child seat tightly into the junction of the car seat back and cushion.

You should also never use a rearward-facing child seat opposite an airbag, though this is fine with forward-facing seats.

Fitting a child safety seat

It is essential that these seats are fitted correctly into place, otherwise their effectiveness in an accident is severely compromised. Yet despite the ease with which modern child safety equipment can be installed, a large number of seats are not fitted correctly. You must follow the fitting instructions to the letter, the first time and on every other occasion that you place the seat in the car.

The majority of child seats are now held in place with the car's own adult seat-belt. Some seats then have their own built-in harness which restrains the child in place, while others make use of the adult belt once more. The intention with all these products is to avoid removing seat cushions, finding concealed mounting points and bolting in attachment straps – you just make use of a safety system which is already there. The other advantage is that it is straightforward to move the seat from one car to another – as long as it is suitable for both models of car.

If you have a car without rear seat-belts it is still possible to buy child seats with their own fastening straps. Fitting is a bit more involved, but as long as you can wield a spanner the job is pretty straightforward. If you do not feel confident doing the job, most garages will do it for you for a small fee.

CHAPTER 9

Day-to-Day Problems

Only the luckiest of drivers go through life without running into a few problems with their day-to-day motoring. Parking, accidents and traffic offences are all difficulties that most of us experience. With a little forethought you should be able to deal with the majority of them with a minimum of hassle.

Parking

Where can you legally park? In the simplest terms, you are entitled to park on public roads where restrictions are not in force, and the situation is not dangerous. You have no right to park on private roads or land, the pavement or verge, even though you may regularly get away with it. But the situation with parking is far from straightforward, so here are a few common problem areas.

On a single yellow line

There will be at least eight hours a day, on at least four days a week, when you cannot park here. A sign at the roadside will tell you the precise restrictions. Outside these hours you can park freely (unless it is potentially dangerous), though if there is no sign telling you the restricted times, you must assume that they apply all the time, even on Sundays and bank holidays.

Remember, too, that these no-parking rules apply not only to the road, but also to the adjacent pavement or verge. The only time you can get away with it is when you are dropping off or picking up passengers or a load.

On a double yellow line

The rules here are exactly the same as for a single yellow line, except that you will find that the restrictions will be longer – quite often the sign next to a double yellow will state 'At any time', indicating that you must never park there (though you can still briefly load and unload).

On a single dashed yellow line

This allows parking for a limited amount of time, perhaps an hour or two. Invariably, you must not return to the same spot within a fixed time, perhaps twice what you were allowed for parking.

By yellow lines across the kerb

These are aimed at delivery vehicles to business premises and restrict the times they are allowed to load or unload. Almost certainly there will already be other restrictions in force where you see these which prevent you from parking freely.

On a 'red route' in London

These specially designated roads in London prohibit any form of parking, even for loading, in order to keep the traffic moving. They are usually confined to the busiest roads, which have been hard hit by rush-hour jams.

Outside your neighbour's house

As long as there are no other restrictions in force, you are entitled to park in the street outside your own or anyone else's house. No one has a divine right to the parking spot in the street outside their home, though to take someone else's 'space' can cause a lot of unnecessary hard feeling.

Prohibited places

There are plenty of places where parking is forbidden except in exceptional circumstances (these have to be truly exceptional, like a breakdown, rather than the need to make an urgent call on a mobile phone, for example):

- on a motorway, except on the hard shoulder in an emergency
- on a pedestrian crossing, or on the zigzag lines on either side
- on the right-hand side of the road at night (except on a one-way street)
- on a clearway (except to drop off or pick up passengers)
- where there are double white lines in the middle of the road – even if one is dashed (except to drop off or pick up passengers or to load)
- in parking areas reserved for residents or disabled drivers
- in a 'disc zone' parking area, unless you display the proper disc
- between 7am and 7pm at the bus stop marked with a wide yellow line
- where it might cause danger to pedestrians, such as near a school entrance, obscuring a traffic sign, on a footpath or cycle path, on or near a level crossing.

Parking penalties

Fines for parking are the most common motoring penalties. There are two major differences in the type of fine you might receive.

A **fixed penalty** will be levied for routine parking offences. You pay a fixed charge, which will vary according to where the offence takes place, and that is the end of the matter. In more serious instances you could be prosecuted for **parking in a dangerous position**. This may be dealt with by a fixed penalty or you could be taken to court, which, if you are found guilty, could result in a fine of up to £1,000 and three penalty points.

You might be less fortunate and get **wheel-clamped**. The London Metropolitan Area is the only region of the UK where wheel-clamping on public roads is carried out. In theory you should not get clamped straight away for a minor parking infringement, but if, for example, you let a parking meter over-run by more than 15 minutes you are fair game. It is impossible to move your car once the clamp has been fitted, so you have to follow the instructions attached to your windscreen to locate the clampers on the telephone, and then pay a 'clamp release fee' once they arrive. This is around £35, though on top of that you have to pay the standard parking fine, which may be up to £60.

Private wheel-clamping is an altogether more contentious matter. Understandably, owners of private car parks get fed up with the general public leaving cars on their property. They may then fit clamps to 'illegally' parked cars, or contract the task out to a private company. Unfortunately, a situation has developed where it seems that areas are being set up so that unsuspecting motorists are caught. The warning signs are small and hidden away, and the fee being asked to release a car can be extortionate – perhaps as high as £200.

Following a court case in Scotland in June 1992, private wheel-clamping has been outlawed there, but in the rest of the UK the law is still a grey area. Where there has been a strong legal case against the clampers, and organisations like the AA have tried to take them to court, the clampers have tended to settle out of court and thus avoid a legal precedent being set. Much pressure has been put on the Government to clarify the situation regarding private clampers, but in the meantime the most sensible advice you can follow is to avoid parking on private land unless you are sure that you have permission.

In many areas of the country your car might be **towed away** or, more likely, lifted on to the back of a lorry and taken to a police pound. This sort of treatment is usually reserved for flagrant offences, such as parking in a dangerous place or repeatedly ignoring parking restrictions. If your car is towed away, the first you will probably know of it is that the car is not where you left it. A call to the local police station should confirm if it has been removed by the police or stolen. If it is in the police pound you then have to make your own way there and pay a hefty fine – something in the region of £100 is common – before your car will be released.

Changes in parking penalties

Most parking violations are criminal offences, which means that if you want to contest a parking ticket you have to attend a magistrates' court. However, from July 1994 the Government de-criminalised parking in London, with the exception of parking on red routes. Instead of fines, errant parking incurs 'penalty charges'. These are administered by the local authority rather than the courts and are treated as a civil offence. Along with these changes in the law many parking schemes are being privatised, with the result that the familiar police-controlled traffic warden is being replaced by a parking attendant working for a private company. It seems likely that this system will be extended into other counties and metropolitan areas of the UK over the coming years.

Until recently you could legally appeal against a parking fine in London on the grounds of mitigating circumstances, if there was a genuinely unavoidable reason that you left your car illegally parked. You might well find your chances of an appeal are now vastly reduced, as mitigating circumstances have no legal basis – it is down to the borough or its contractor to act as judge and jury. If you cannot settle a dispute, you can appeal to the independent Parking Adjudicator Officer.

Parking accidents

Damage caused to cars while parking is extremely annoying, the more so because it is usually the result of a moment's carelessness. The person causing the damage should always try to locate the owner of the other vehicle or, at the very least, leave a note on the windscreen advising them of the circumstances and a contact name and address.

There is no real defence for hitting a parked car. Even if it were badly parked, the driver of the car manoeuvring past should appreciate the difficulties involved and, if necessary, abandon this manoeuvre for an alternative.

MOTORING OFFENCES

Usually it is the police who will initiate a prosecution against you. The common exception is when a local authority pursues you through the courts to recover unpaid parking fines. It is the norm to be warned before being prosecuted, either verbally or in writing. Whatever happens, the police *must* start proceedings within six months of the alleged offence, except in exceptional circumstances.

If you do get a warning that you might be prosecuted (as opposed to the notice of prosecution itself) a grovelling letter to the Chief Constable is always worth a try. You should express considerable regret and say you will endeavour not to repeat the same mistake again. This may work in minor cases, but is a less promising avenue for more serious offences. If you are being prosecuted for more than one offence, you could also write asking whether the police might drop the lesser charge if you admitted to the more serious one.

Fixed penalties

A number of offences are dealt with by the 'fixed penalty' system. The traditional one has been illegal parking, but the number has been extended to include other infringements, such as speeding, failing to display a tax disc, crossing a red traffic light, and having a defective vehicle.

These are not dealt with by on-the-spot fines, as you might receive in some other countries. If you are given a fixed penalty you do not have to part with any money there and then, but you will be given a ticket which gives you the opportunity to pay a fixed fine within the next 28 days. This means you can still plead 'not guilty' if you want the case to go to court, though you run the risk of ending up further out of pocket if you lose the case. Fixed penalties will not be applied in *all* circumstances. If your offence is considered a serious one, the police might decide that the case should be heard through the courts.

With some fixed-penalty offences you pay the fine and that is the end of the matter. Others, notably speeding, will add penalty points to your licence. When that happens, the police will take away your licence at the time (assuming that you have it with you) and give you a receipt which will cover you for driving your car in the meantime. If you do not have your licence, you will have to take it to a police station within the next few days.

The idea behinds the fixed penalty is that it cuts down on an awful lot of paperwork and bureaucracy. It is quick and simple to deal with, which benefits the police, magistrates and, indeed, many motorists.

Endorsements

Many motoring offences are endorsable, which means that they could result in disqualification from driving for the person who builds up a bad driving record. For every 'endorsable' offence (there are many, like parking, which are not endorsable), you will be given a number of penalty points. For a minor speeding offence, for example, you may get three points. If you accumulate twelve points or more over a three-year period, you will almost certainly be prohibited from driving for at least six months, though this could be a year or more in the most serious cases.

For more serious motoring offences it is possible to lose your licence even though you have not accumulated enough penalty points. If you have a clean licence, yet are caught speeding at 120 mph, it is quite likely that you will be banned from driving even though a speeding offence normally carries a maximum penalty of six points. It is likely that such a disqualification will be for a shorter period than six months, however. In the most serious of offences, such as causing death by dangerous driving, a driver can also be imprisoned.

Fines and penalties

The fixed-penalty system is straightforward. For penalty point offences and parking on a 'red route' in London the fine is £40. Illegal parking elsewhere in London brings a £30 fine, and all other offences £20. If you do not pay up within 28 days (or request a court hearing), the penalty is increased by 50 per cent.

If your case is heard by a court, the level of fine, whether you get disqualified or even sent to prison, is down to the judge's or magistrates' discretion, according to certain guidelines.

Guilty or not guilty?

The majority of motoring cases are dealt with through the magistrates' courts, and many motorists plead guilty for mixed reasons. First, many obviously are guilty, but others who feel there may be some doubt, or even those who feel strongly that

Table of penalties

Offence	Penalty points	Maximum fine	Disqualification?	Prison?
Speeding	3 to 6	£1,000	possible	no
No MOT	none	£1,000	no	no
Not wearing seat-belt	none	£500	no	no
Stopping unnecessarily on motorway hard shoulder	2 to 4	£2,500	no	no
Light traffic offences	3	£1,000	possible	no
Careless driving	3 to 9	£2,500	possible	no
No insurance	6 to 8	£5,000	possible	no
Driving when disqualified	6	£5,000	possible	up to 6 months (12 in Scotland)
Failing to stop after an accident	5 to 10	£5,000	possible	up to 6 months
Drink-driving	12	£5,000	12 months	up to 6 months
Failure to provide a specimen for drink-drive analysis	12	£5,000	12 months	up to 6 months
Causing death under influence of drink or drugs	12	Unlimited	2 years minimum	up to 10 years
Dangerous driving	12	Unlimited	yes, variable	up to 2 years
Causing death by dangerous driving	12	Unlimited	2 years minimum	up to 10 years

they are not guilty, follow the same path because it reduces the hassle and cost involved in pleading not guilty. There is also the undoubted difficulty of convincing a court to take your word against that of a policeman or policewoman.

Should you decide to plead guilty there are special reasons for asking a court not to disqualify you, if that option is on the cards. You will probably need the help of a solicitor to get you on the right track, but, briefly, you are looking for a *special reason* which amounts to a mitigating or extenuating circumstance.

If, however, you do decide to plead not guilty, you should take legal advice. A solicitor will be able to give you a much better idea of your chances of acquittal and tell you whether you are wasting your time and money going through with the court case.

ACCIDENTS, AND HOW TO DEAL WITH THEM

A road accident is always a traumatic time for those involved. At the very least it is going to cost someone some money, with injuries a possibility. Given the possibility of an accident, a little thought now can mean you are better prepared to deal with one should it occur.

The law lays down a number of actions you must take. If there is any injury to a person or animal – horse, cattle, ass, mule, sheep, pig, goat or dog, though not cat – or any damage to property or vehicle, you *must* stop. Anyone then having reasonable grounds can demand your name and address, and you can demand the same of other people. They, in turn, must give you that information – to refuse is an offence.

If it is impossible to give your name and address – perhaps because no one else is around – then you must give it to a policeman or at a police station within the next 24 hours. If someone has been injured, then no matter what, the accident has to be reported to the police.

Ten-point guide to handling an accident

1 Stop your car, in a safe place if at all possible.

2 See if anyone is injured. If so, call for help immediately – if not yourself, then get another motorist or bystander to do it.

3 Take the name and address of any witnesses. These are people not directly involved in the accident but who may have seen it, and the circumstances leading up to it. Witnesses are often forgotten about in the heat of the moment but can make a big difference to any prosecution or insurance claim at a later date.
4 Take the name and address of the other driver(s) involved in the accident. You will also need to get details of their insurance company, which they may or may not have with them. Look for some proof that they are who they claim to be.
5 Note down the registration number of the other car(s) involved, as well as the make, model and colour.
6 Note the date and time of the accident. Draw a quick sketch of the accident site, showing the position of the cars before and after the accident.
7 Make a record of the weather conditions, and the type of road surface – was it slippery, for example?
8 See if the other driver appears to be under the influence of drink, and get a witness to agree with your diagnosis.
9 Never admit liability for the accident, or sign any statement unless asked to by a police officer. Your insurance company will deal with all this, and you may compromise the case if you make admissions now.
10 *Do not lose your cool.* Be polite and patient at all times – it will not make any difference to the outcome if you rant and rave at the others involved, and you will forget to cover the more important matters outlined above.

Quite often the police will not be interested in making a prosecution in a road traffic accident unless it is serious or there is personal injury involved. You may even find that the police refuse to attend to a minor accident unless it is causing an obstruction or fighting has broken out. You should insist on the police coming to the scene, however, if you feel that the other driver has been drinking, as this will certainly support your case.

After the accident

If your car is driveable after the accident, you should give it a look-over to ensure that it is both safe and legal and then make your way home or to a garage. If the car cannot be driven, the police will almost certainly make arrangements for a contracted breakdown service to come to collect it and deposit it in a safe pound until it can be repaired. It is unlikely you will be able to recover your car from this pound until you have at least paid the breakdown company for its bill. Normally this will be dealt with by your insurance company; but if you have only third party, fire and theft insurance, you will have to pay the bill yourself.

Get your insurance company involved at the earliest opportunity. It will be used to dealing with this distressing situation, and should be able to guide you through the paperwork as well as being able to provide valuable advice. Your insurance may, for example, provide for a 'free' hire car for a week or two while your car is out of action. If not, your insurer should be able to advise you whether, if you hired a car at your own expense, you could recover the cost from the other parties involved in the accident.

Strictly speaking, if you are the innocent party in a car accident, you have every right to claim additional expenses from the guilty driver. By law you should take every opportunity to mitigate these expenses – that is, keep them as low as possible. Do not, for example, insist on hiring a very expensive car when a cheap one would do. Unfortunately, the cause of many accidents is far from black and white, so you may run the risk of building up costs which you end up having to pay for yourself.

A key aspect of all post-accident dealings is to let your insurance company handle all the correspondence. When you receive a letter from the other party, or his or her insurers, send it along unanswered to your insurers. They are the ones who will be dealing with the claim and the final payment, and in the end it is up to the insurers to sort out the details.

CHAPTER 10

Taking Your Car Abroad

The Channel Tunnel has raised the awareness of just how easy it is to take your car abroad. For those not keen on sea travel there is now a real alternative that is both quick and easy to use. Whichever method you choose, it still remains one of the most expensive stretches of water in the world to get across, but if you are prepared to compromise by travelling outside the peak times, you can easily halve the cost of your trip to France.

France, of course, is not the only gateway for you and your car into Europe. Ireland, Spain, Belgium, Holland, Denmark and Norway are all accessible by direct ferry route from the UK, and if you do not live in the bottom half of England may well be the more convenient stepping-off point. And these alternative destinations need not cost you any more. How much you are charged on a ferry seems to have less to do with the distance you travel than with the demand for services on a particular route.

Travelling on the Continent with your own car has much going for it. If you have a family, it is almost certainly the cheapest way of getting around, and you have the convenience of going exactly where *you* want to go, when you want to go there. The growth in the number of good-value camping holidays on offer in France and other nearby European countries has seen a large number of people trying out European motoring for the first time, with little ill-effect.

The major obstacle you will encounter, of course, is that everyone else (apart from the Irish) drives on the right-hand-side of the road. Thirty or forty years ago this was considered a serious concern, a matter which required some particular skills and experience. Today it is accepted that driving on the right in a right-hand-drive car, while not immediately straightforward, can quickly be mastered with some patience and care. It should certainly not be a factor which puts you off European motoring.

There are other differences you will come across, apart from on which side of the road you point your car. The rules at roundabouts may differ from those in the UK, and parking may be treated in a totally different way. These rules will vary from country to country, but you will be able to get a synopsis from the motoring organisations or the ferry companies. The channel ports have offices which can provide this type of information.

Before you do go, you will need to check out a few important details which could make for a more successful, stress-free trip. Despite the breaking down of European barriers, driving abroad is not the same as driving to Dover but twice as far. You need to think carefully about additional matters which might cause difficulties while you are away from home.

PREPARING YOUR CAR

Needless to say, your car should be in excellent mechanical condition before you take it abroad. While most cars available for sale in the UK are sold throughout Europe, and so present a good chance of finding a garage to fix a problem if you have one, few people want to waste time having their car repaired while they are away on holiday.

Mechanical checks

There are routine checks which everyone should regularly make on their car, but few do. Is the water in the radiator and washer bottle topped up? Check the oil level. Pump up the tyres. Most cars require extra air pressure in the tyres when travelling fully loaded – your handbook will tell you. Check the spare tyre pressure too, and that you have the tools necessary to change a wheel if you get a puncture.

If your car is due for a service shortly before you go tell the garage about your trip so it can pay particular attention to the requirements. Even if your car is not due for a trip to the workshop, you will find that in the late spring and summer many garages offer a special 'holiday service'. This will probably cover all the important points that you would check at home, plus maybe an oil change and a check of all the lights, brakes and so on. The cost is rarely high, and worth having if you do not feel up to the job yourself. Look in your local newspaper for garages offering this service, and compare what each offers with the cost. The inclusion of an engine oil and filter change is worth £15 to £20 more.

Fuel

It is only in Eastern Europe that finding the right grade of fuel might sometimes be a little difficult. That means the majority of petrol stations will sell unleaded petrol, leaded (4*) petrol and diesel. The availability of super unleaded petrol is more varied, so if your car is one of the few which requires this, check with the tourist office of the countries you are intending to visit, or the AA or RAC (see Addresses).

As in the UK, fuel prices vary greatly according to where you buy. In France, for example, fuel is significantly more expensive in motorway service areas than it is at a supermarket – if anything, the difference between these two types of outlet is greater than at home. Petrol is anyway much more expensive in France, while diesel fuel is around two-thirds the cost of petrol – so it pays to own a diesel car if you do a lot of motoring in France. The situation is not the same in Germany, however, where fuel costs are broadly similar to those in the UK.

A rule of thumb is for owners of petrol cars to fill up before they catch their ferry. Those with a diesel should certainly wait until they get to France; those going to other countries can take their choice. Finally, it is important not to over-fill your fuel tank before going on a ferry or train, for safety's sake.

Badges, lights and things

Different countries take different views on having a country sticker on the back of a car, but bear in mind that you can be fined entering a country without the correct identification on your car. To be safe you should always use a GB badge. There is no need to pay for it – as one will undoubtedly arrive with your ferry tickets or with your holiday booking.

As British cars are right-hand-drive, the headlights dip towards the middle of the road – and oncoming traffic – when driving on the right-hand side. You can correct this with a simple-to-use headlamp beam adjuster kit, which consists of some pre-cut black patches which are stuck to the headlamps. These cut out the portion of the light which points across the road, and though they reduce the output of your headlights a little, it is not enough to worry about. Many cars in France still have yellow headlamps. These are no longer compulsory, though you can buy bottles of removable yellow paint at car accessory shops to tint your lights if you wish.

Most cars have a mirror mounted on the front passenger door. This is very useful when driving abroad as it allows you to judge what is going on behind you when you want to overtake. If your car does not have one you can buy a door mirror for a few pounds. Some are clip-on, which are particularly ease to fit.

A first-aid kit is a sensible item to carry around in your car in the UK, and compulsory in a few other countries.

Spare parts

There is a small body of opinion which recommends you carry a broad range of spare parts in the car so that most eventualities can be dealt with should they occur. You can even rent boxes of spares from the AA and RAC, collect them at the port of departure and pay for any bit you use while you are away.

This may seem like a good idea for an older model, for which spares might be hard to find in Europe, but is largely unnecessary if you have a reasonably modern car. You would be better off spending your money on decent Continental breakdown insurance so that if something does go wrong, the parts will be shipped out to you quickly from the UK should they prove difficult to locate in the country where you are stranded.

By law, however, certain countries oblige motorists, including foreign tourists, to carry a number of items in their car (see chart opposite).

Items you should carry with you

	Warning triangle	First-aid kit	Fire extinguisher	Spare set of bulbs
Austria	✓	✓		
Belgium	✓			
Denmark	✓			
France	✓			✓
Germany	✓	✓		✓
Greece	✓	✓	✓	
Holland	✓			
Italy	✓			
Luxembourg	✓			
Norway				
Portugal	✓			
Spain				✓
Sweden	✓			
Switzerland	✓	✓		

THE PAPERWORK

As much as we are told that Europe is now one big community, with border restrictions being removed, you still cannot just jump in your car and simply take it to Europe. It is essential that you cover yourself by dealing with the following bits of paperwork.

Passport

This is still an essential requirement. Though it is quite common for European border officials to wave through British cars without even a glance at your passports, you are almost certain to need it when you get back to England.

Car insurance

All UK car insurance policies automatically provide the cover required by law in EC countries, plus some others. The drawback is that this level of cover is very minimal, covering you against the worst possible eventualities, such as being sued for hundreds of thousands of pounds for damages, but not the things that are likely to happen more often, like damage to your own car.

It is still advisable, therefore, to ask your insurer for a Green Card, an international motor insurance certificate which is recognised everywhere and provides the same level of cover as you have at home. You may get this free or you may have to pay an additional charge of perhaps £15 to £25 for a two-week trip. If you make more than one trip abroad each year, it is worth checking out car insurance companies which do not charge extra for foreign cover, as this can have a considerable effect on your overall premiums.

Driving licence

You should always take your full UK driving licence with you. Note that a provisional licence does not count, and even if you have passed your test, in some countries (Austria, Belgium, France, Italy, Luxembourg, Holland, Spain and Switzerland) you will not be allowed to drive if you are under 18 years of age.

The UK licence is recognised almost everywhere, but it is advisable to get an International Driving Permit (from the AA or RAC – see Addresses) if you are travelling to Eastern Europe or Greece, Portugal or Spain. This is easily recognised by the police and may help things along if you get into difficulties.

Bail bond

In Spain even a minor traffic offence can result in serious repercussions, and you may be required to lodge a bond with the police before they will release you from custody. You can get a 'bail bond' from most insurance companies, which guarantees payment of any subsequent fine. You will still have to pay the fine from your own pocket eventually, however.

Registration documents

Another requirement is that you must be able to prove that you are entitled to drive your car. The Vehicle Registration Document is accepted as proof of this. If it is a company or hire car then have a word with your fleet manager or the hire company, who will give you proof sufficient for the trip.

Breakdown and personal insurance

Dare you travel without car breakdown cover? Few people seem to travel abroad without Continental breakdown cover for their car, yet cars are more reliable than ever. Today, the Europeanisation of car models means that it is unlikely that you would have trouble getting spare parts for most cars abroad, but it is still helpful to be able to call on an English-speaking operative who can take the sting out of a breakdown. There are half a dozen major operators in the field, all offering the equivalent of their UK breakdown service with enhancements like an alternative car if yours cannot be fixed immediately, and a limited amount of cover for unexpected hotel bills.

The big advantage of taking out this sort of cover is that if something does go wrong you have a friendly English-speaking voice on the other end of the telephone who will help. Whether it is an accident or a breakdown, your operator will arrange for someone local to come to your assistance, and deal with any problems along the way. Bills for repairs can be expensive abroad, and it is very difficult to argue about suspected overcharging if you do not have a grasp of the language. A Continental breakdown service will help reduce the worry.

All the major UK breakdown companies – AA, RAC, National Breakdown, Britannia, Autohome, Mondial and Europ Assistance – offer at least one package covering foreign motoring. You will find that there are enhancements too, at extra cost, which provide a better level of cover. Whether you really need any of this is largely a personal decision – the cost can be £40 to £90 for a fortnight in Europe for the car alone, though National Breakdown offers up to 17 days 'free' Continental cover with its more comprehensive UK schemes.

Whenever you book a trip abroad you will inevitably be offered some form of personal insurance. You are rarely forced to take this and you can shop around or roll the whole thing in with your car breakdown cover. There is a reciprocal arrangement for health care in EC countries, which means that you are entitled to a certain amount of free care; but most people still find it more convenient to buy a personal insurance package which includes cover for health as well as cover for luggage and other items.

Continental breakdown cover

1994 rates

	Car age years	17 days' cover	Contact
AA 5-Star	up to 10	£45.50[1]	
	10+	£70.50[1]	(0256) 55295
Bishopsgate	up to 10	£40.95	(0703) 644455
Britannia	up to 7	£42.00[2]	
	7 to 13	£52.50[2]	
	13+	£71.50[2]	(0484) 514848
Europ Assistance	up to 16	£41.50	(0444) 442211
Mondial	up to 10	£44.00	
	10 to 15	£66.00	081-681 2525
National Breakdown	up to 10	£43.00	
	10 to 15	£86.00	(0532) 393666
RAC	up to 10	£55.95[1]	
	10+	£88.90	(0800) 550055

[1] +£3 for non-members

[2] +£5 for non-members

PLANNING

Getting there

The choice of route to the Continent, even before the Channel Tunnel was opened, was never an easy one, particularly if your destination was France. The difficulty lies in the compromise you have to make between cost, driving time and convenience. If you are happy to drive a long distance, you will get further quicker by sticking to the roads rather than the sea as far as possible. That means taking a short ferry crossing, and that means going via Dover.

Travelling via Dover has other advantages. The roads to it are pretty good, and the popular destination on the other side, Calais, has a motorway running right to the doorstep of the port. There are many ferries making the Dover–Calais run, with Sealink and P&O offering, between them, over 35 trips a day in peak times as well as the hovercraft and jetfoils of Hoverspeed. So if you turn up early or late for your booked crossing, there is every chance that you use could another from the same company.

Such flexibility is far more difficult if you choose one of the long crossings: there may be only one or two crossings a day. And as it is vital for most passengers to arrive on time for their booked crossing, you may find it more difficult to get on a boat if you miss your slot. Ships are much slower than cars, too, so you will not necessarily save a great deal of time.

The advantages of the long crossings are undeniable, however. They may well get you much closer to your final destination than the short hop to Calais or Boulogne. If you are going to Brittany, for example, many of the favourite spots are just a matter of hours from the western French ports of St Malo and Cherbourg. Access from the UK to these ports is from points along the south coast, generally Portsmouth, Southampton, Plymouth or Portsmouth, which are easier to get to than Dover from much of the UK.

The cost factor is one which you have to balance in your own mind. Surprisingly, the price of travelling from England to France can be much the same whether you take a 75-minute crossing to Calais or a six-hour one to Cherbourg. But arriving in Cherbourg in the late afternoon does not give you much daylight travelling time in France. Instead, many choose a night crossing on the boat, which gets them into port for around 6.30am, allowing plenty of driving time (if you need it) that day. Unfortunately, night crossings on the long routes tend to be more expensive, and you are unlikely to get much sleep unless you book a cabin, which can add £100 or more to the final bill.

If you want to travel to a country other than France, you will find there is little, if any, choice of route and ferry operator. You should always bear in mind how much sleep you normally need and whether you are likely to get it on a ship. You may find that instead of paying the extra for a night crossing and cabin, a daylight journey and a motel at the other end would be far more comfortable and no more expensive.

As for the Channel Tunnel, that was yet to be opened to public traffic as we went to press.

Motorail

If you would like to have your car with you abroad, but do not fancy huge hauls on foreign motorways, then the motorail may be the answer. This departs from Boulogne for destinations in the south of France, Bordeaux and Milan. You drive to Dover, take an afternoon ferry to Boulogne where you drive the short distance to the station for your car to be loaded on the train. You then retire to your reserved seats for a picnic and a night's sleep – first class is said to be worth the extra cost.

Motorail is an expensive way to travel compared with driving long distances before stopping overnight. But if your car travel is normally at a more sedate pace, and you stop in a hotel or two on the way, it could well be that the economic argument for the train is a reasonable one.

Route planning

Anyone who can read a map should have little difficulty in finding their way to their destination in Europe. There are plenty of helpful European road atlases in the bookshops. If you want to cover great distances in a day, say 400 miles plus, you have no real alternative to sticking to the motorways. French 'N' roads may look straight on the maps but the small towns along the way drastically cut back your average speed.

If speed is not the only ingredient in your journey, however, then you might well benefit from a purpose-designed route. The AA and RAC offer these for a modest fee, and will plan a route for you which will be as scenic as you like, as well as providing information about the places you visit along the way. This is the sort of information it is very hard to come across unless you know someone with first-hand experience.

Motorway tolls

In several European countries you will be charged to use the motorway. The costs can be steep: Calais to Geneva, for example, will set you back over £30 one-way, which is likely to exceed the cost of your fuel. The other side of the coin is that the over-crowding we know so well in the UK is less of a problem, although holiday weekends can still be bad. Cash is the favourite method of payment, though you can use a credit card in France and Spain. In Switzerland you have to buy an annual 'Vignette' to use the motorways. This costs around £15 – you could well be stopped by the police as you enter the country and forced to pay on the spot, so if you do not intend to use the motorways, cross the border on an ordinary road.

Speed limits

You will not get away with speeding just because you are a foreigner (see page 148 for limits). On-the-spot fines are normal almost everywhere. An all-too-easy digression on the French Autoroute will set you back over £100. If you cannot pay there and then, you will be taken to a bank to get some money!

Last-minute advice

The Foreign Office travel advisory bureau (071-270 4129 or 4179) gives advice to travellers on the advisability of travelling to any area of the world. This may be of help if you are thinking of driving to parts of the Balkans, for example. Likewise, the motoring organisations may be able to provide assistance on the same subject.

	Motorways mph	Major roads mph	Towns mph
Austria	81	62	31
Belgium	74	56	37
Denmark	62	50	31
France	81	68	31
Germany	no limit	62/81	31
Greece	62	50	31
Holland	74	50	31
Italy	81	56	31
Luxembourg	74	56	37
Norway	56	49	31
Portugal	74	56	37
Spain	74	56/62	37
Sweden	68	43/56	31
Switzerland	74	50	31

Security

One of the worst things which can happen while you are on a motoring holiday is for your car to be broken into and your valuables stolen. It will be traumatic, at the least, to find that your passport and travellers' cheques have been stolen, so it is vital that you take some reasonable precautions. Wherever possible you should keep your most important documents on your person, rather than leaving them in the car. Avoid parking your car in a vulnerable area – a busy, well-lit road is better than a dark side-street where thieves can attack the car unnoticed. Theft of car radios is as common in some European countries as it is at home – Italy has a terrible reputation – so remove your radio or the fascia if it has this facility.

If you do suffer a theft you should report the matter to the police. They should be able to give you the name of the nearest British Consulate, which will be able to help with passport problems. Travellers' cheques can be replaced pretty readily, and credit card companies can be telephoned in the UK for help and advice on lost cards. Remember to read the rules and advice supplied with travellers' cheques and credit cards so that you know what to do should the worst happen.

TAKING A CARAVAN ABROAD

Caravanning abroad is a popular though not necessarily an economical option. The ferry company will probably want to charge you extra (though there are many good deals if you travel outside of the peak times), the motorway tolls are higher and campsite fees can easily reach £25 a night. But caravanning, of course, gives you unrivalled flexibility and is, for many, a way of life.

A few preparations should be made before you take your caravan abroad. First it should have had a mechanical service, so the chassis, brakes, coupling and lighting are all in good condition. Check that the spare wheel is OK and that the van has a chassis identification plate – vital in many countries (if it has not, the AA or RAC can help).

You will need an extra GB badge for the back of the caravan and an extending mirror for the driver's and passenger's side – obligatory in Italy or Denmark.

Caravans are banned from certain city or town centres, notably Paris. Good route planning is even more vital than it is with cars, so a custom route for a caravan from one of the motoring organisations will help you avoid the most difficult roads.

The UK speed limit of 60 mph with a caravan in tow does not hold in the rest of Europe, where each country has its own requirements (see page 150).

	Speed limit with caravan (mph)
Austria	62, Tyrol 50
Denmark	43
France	same as cars
Germany	50
Holland	50
Italy	50, 62 motorways
Luxembourg	43, 56 motorways
Norway	50
Portugal	43, 56 motorways
Spain	43, 50 motorways
Sweden	43
Switzerland	50

CHAPTER 11

MAKING THE MOST OF YOUR COMPANY CAR

The company car plays an enormously important part in many employees' lives. The objective here is not to to argue the rights and wrongs of the system and the attitudes to it, but to help you to make the most of the company car opportunity if you are lucky enough to get it.

As every driver of a car supplied with a job knows only too well, there is a downside as well. The tax on the benefit has increased steeply in recent years. Then in 1994 the way in which the tax was calculated was changed completely, so that some drivers were suddenly better or worse off than before. It means that, more than ever, there is a good case for considering whether that posh executive model is really worth the money you eventually have to pay for it.

MAJOR FACTORS IN YOUR CHOICE OF COMPANY CAR

Just what you are entitled to in the way of a car will vary greatly according to your company's policy. Some will tell you that you will drive a white Vauxhall Cavalier 1.6 LS hatchback. Others may give you a list of half a dozen similar models from which to choose. Or you may be 'given' a sum of money and sent off to make your own choice.

According to the annual Tolley Survey of Company Car Schemes, 43 per cent of representatives are given a limited range of cars to choose from, 28 per cent are given a free choice within a price range and 27 per cent are allocated a specific model of car. As your seniority within the company rises, so does your chance of a 'free choice' of car, within certain set limits.

But despite the apparent freedom of choice, few companies are in reality prepared to make such a wholehearted generous gesture towards their employees. For while it is easy to pick a dozen different models costing within £100 of any pre-set spending limit, the real cost to the company will be very different. The big problems are depreciation and running costs. One £15,000 car will be worth £8,000 in three years' time, another used under identical conditions will be worth just £5,000. The same applies to the running costs of cars, with vastly different servicing and insurance expenses masking the similarity in their original price.

Do not feel hard done by if your company offers you only the choice of three or four cars, or restricts the choice by some other means. A favourite device is to offer cars based upon their leasing cost. You may, for example, be allowed to choose any car up to a limit of £400 a month. This is the figure your company is prepared to pay a leasing or contract hire company for its cars (if it does not buy them outright), and it takes most of the awkward factors like servicing and depreciation into account. It is a reasonable route to ask your company to explore if it is being stingy on the choice of car, though many are still extremely stubborn about making changes for fear of upsetting the status quo.

Given some freedom of choice, just how do you go about making the final decision? While accepting that most company car drivers aim to get a car they would not normally consider if they were paying from their own pocket, you should look at the following:

- does the car meet the day-to-day needs of your job (your company will almost certainly make sure it does, even if you do not)?
- does it meet the needs of your private use?

- how much company car taxation will you have to pay?
- how much is your private fuel going to cost over the year?
- if you pay for private fuel, would you be better off with a diesel?
- is there a better alternative to having the company car, such as getting a pay rise and buying your own?

You can make your own judgments on your company and domestic motoring needs; below, the tax and other considerations are dealt with in detail.

THE CURRENT TAX SITUATION

Virtually everyone with a company car is taxed on it. The only exceptions are those on extremely low salaries, though company directors are excluded from this. In addition, there is a second tax to pay if your company meets *any* of the fuel costs for your private motoring. The way in which your company car is taxed was dramatically revised in April 1994. We have not covered the old system here as it is now irrelevant, except for those who want to work out the difference between the old and new rates.

How much tax will you pay?

The principle of taxing an employee's company car has not changed, just the method of working out how much is to be paid. In both cases a notional amount is added to your salary. Say you earn £20,000 a year. Your car may be calculated to be 'worth' another £4,000 a year, which means that you will be paying income tax on £24,000 instead of £20,000. As employees earning this level of salary pay income tax at 25 per cent, then the company car will in reality be costing them 25 per cent of £4,000, or £1,000 a year. If, however, you earn considerably more and your salary falls into the 40 per cent income tax band, then you will pay 40 per cent of £4,000, or £1,600 a year to run exactly the same car.

The complicated part is working out the worth, or 'cash equivalent', of the car. The calculation goes like this:

- take the car manufacturer's or importer's published list price for the car at the time it was first registered (not necessarily the same as when you started driving it, or the current price)
- add the delivery charge and the cost of any extras which were fitted before the car was passed over to you (excluding a mobile telephone)
- calculate 35 per cent of this total figure – this is the initial 'cash equivalent' value of your company car.

Factors which reduce your company car taxation

It is easy to work out from the above that a car which is listed at £15,000 including delivery and extras will have a 'cash equivalent' of £5,250 (35 per cent of £15,000) per annum, which translates to a tax burden of £1,313 for those paying 25 per cent income tax, £2,100 for those on 40 per cent. There are several ways in which this figure can be substantially reduced:

- if you drive between 2,500 and 18,000 miles a year on business, the amount is reduced by one-third
- if you drive over 18,000 business miles a year, the 'cash equivalent' is reduced by two-thirds
- if your company car is 4 years old or more at the end of the year of assessment, then the 'cash equivalent' is reduced by a further third.

Classic cars

Classic cars are a special case. If they are under 15 years old, you will be charged on the above basis, that is you will get your age-related reduction. Once they reach that age, however, their value is re-assessed and if it is deemed to be greater than £15,000 then you will be taxed on that revised value. That could make a significant difference to a car which cost perhaps £3,000 when it was new but had increased in value to £16,000 by the time it was 15 years old. When 14, the 'cash equivalent' would be £703 for a low-mileage user, after which it would rise to £3,750!

Tax on free fuel

Many company car drivers get the petrol or diesel they use for private motoring paid for by their employer. This very useful perk is also taxed, but importantly it bears no relation to how much free fuel you get.

If your company pays for *any* free fuel for your car, you have to pay a fixed amount – the 'fuel scale charge'. This is added to your salary in the same way as the car 'cash equivalent' and is as follows:

Engine capacity	Scale charge	
	Petrol	Diesel
1400cc or less	£640	£580
1401cc to 2000cc	£810	£580
more than 2000cc	£1200	£750

Note that there are no reductions applicable to these figures, which apply to the 1994–5 tax year and may increase in the future.

Points to Watch For

Car telephones

If you have a telephone installed in your company car, £200 will be 'added' to your salary and taxed at either 25 per cent or 40 per cent. You can get around this tax by reimbursing your employer for the cost of any private calls – or not making any private calls at all. Receiving reverse-charge calls does not count!

Accessories

Accessories fitted to the car before you take delivery are added automatically to the list price of the car. If they are added after you took delivery of the car *and* they have a list price of at least £100 *and* they were fitted after 31 July 1993, they are also added to the list price of the car in order to calculate the cash equivalent.

Lower-paid employees

You can escape tax on your company car if your 'remuneration package' is worth under £8,500 a year. That is made up of your salary (after pension contributions) and business expenses, as well as the 'cash equivalent' of your company car. Very few people could conceivably qualify for this. Directors are not allowed this option.

Upper limit

After strong complaints from the likes of Rolls-Royce and Aston Martin, sales of which would have been affected by exceedingly severe rises in personal taxation for company car users, a ceiling of £80,000 was put on the value of the list price of new cars for the purposes of calculating the cash equivalent value.

Business mileage

When working out your annual business mileage you are not allowed to include travel to and from work. But if you go directly from home to a business location away from your normal course of business, you can count it as business mileage as long as the overall journey is shorter than going via your normal place of work.

Second company car

If you have two company cars you will find yourself charged at the full 35 per cent, with only a one-third reduction if you use this car for over 18,000 business miles annually.

WAYS TO SAVE ON YOUR TAX

In real terms, the amount employees have been taxed on their company cars has increased steadily over the years. Originally, by providing an employee with a car the company was exploiting a tax loophole. Needless to say, once a large number of people started to benefit from this loophole efforts were made to close it.

The Government says that there will not be any further need to increase taxation on company cars in the future because, as the tax is now linked to the new price of cars and as the prices inexorably rise, so will the amount of tax the Treasury gathers. (Fuel tax is a different matter and is likely to continue to rise in real terms by 5 per cent each year.) With a degree of stability in the system, then, it is a good time to look at ways of reducing your tax burden.

Downsizing

This is the industry buzz-word for choosing a smaller car than the one you have. In reality, of course, you need to choose a car which is both *cheaper* than the one you are currently running, and cheaper now than your current car was when it was first registered. The current system means that tax on your company car will be stable for the three or four years you run it, and then almost certainly will increase with the rise in new car prices over that period. So no matter what, you are certainly going to have to pay an increased amount of tax every time your company car is routinely replaced with a similar one. Downsizing may save you money, or may just mean that you do not pay any more than before.

Savings on downsizing

For every £1,000 off the list price of the car	You save annually 25% taxpayer	40% taxpayer
Up to 2,500 miles annually	£88	£140
2,500 –18,000 miles	£58	£93
over 18,000 miles	£29	£47

The major factor is always the list price of the car when it is registered. If you are in the 25 per cent income tax band, and fall into the typical 2,500–18,000 annual business miles bracket, to save £500 a year on your final tax bill you will have to choose a car which is around £8,500 cheaper than your current one. So if you run a £19,500 Rover 820 Si, you would have to drop to a cheaper Rover 214 to make a £500 saving. If, however, you pay 40 per cent income tax, then you would have to drop by £5,350 in car value to save that £500 – from the big Rover to a high-specification Rover 400.

Contributing towards the cost of your company car

The rules take into account any contribution you make towards the cost of your company car. The amount you contribute will be knocked off the list price of the car when making the calculations. A limit of £5,500 applies, however.

Running a used car

To make a difference to your tax levels, a used car must be at least four years old at the end of the year of assessment. That does not mean that you have to buy a used car – you automatically become entitled to this reduction even if you have run the car from new. If you are not a high-mileage driver, you might consider asking your employer if you could keep your current car for longer or change your current one for a low-mileage 3- or 4-year-old. As the fourth birthday only has to occur in the current tax year, a car first registered in March will become eligible for the reduced rate when it is 3 years and 1 month old.

Watch your mileage

It may seem trite to mention it, but do make a note of the mileage at the beginning of the tax year (5 April) and then record your business mileage over the coming year. It would be foolish to miss out on significant tax reductions by under-running your annual business mileage by a small amount, when an extra journey by car instead of rail would have taken you over the 2,500 or 18,000 break point.

CAR OR CASH?

More companies than ever are prepared to offer employees entitled to a company car the opportunity instead to take an increase in salary. With the amount you are taxed on your company car now said to be close to its real value to you, the argument for having one as a tax dodge is quickly slipping away.

There will always be a body of people, like representatives, who really need a company car on a day-to-day basis for their job, and are unlikely to benefit from a cash-for-car scheme. For others, particularly perk users who need their car on business only a limited amount, a switch may be a good idea.

The equation is never an easy one, however, for it is all too easy to overlook the hidden cost of running a car which your company has always paid for. Tyres, servicing, unexpected repairs to major items, a hire car when yours is in the garage or off the road through an accident, insurance for business use are all factors covered or at least budgeted for by your company fleet manager. They would have to be taken on board by you if you opted for the cash instead. This, of course, assumes that you then buy a car to replace your company one. There will be, however, many employees who find that they do not really need the car in the first place – particularly if there is already one in the household.

If your company does allow you the choice, you must weigh up the figures very carefully. A middle-of-the-road company car, say a Vauxhall Cavalier 2-litre GLS, may be costing you in real terms £800 a year in taxation. If your company then offered you a pay increase of £3,200 a year instead of the car, you would pay the same additional tax – £800 – if you fell into the 25 per cent income tax band. That means you would have an additional £2,400 a year, or £200 a month, in your pocket to use to finance a car. It does not take much to work out that this would hardly finance the cost of buying and running an Astra, let alone a reasonable Cavalier. So you need to be very careful when making your decision.

One of the advantages a company has is that because it is dealing with cars in bulk, it can get economies of scale when buying and maintaining the fleet. These opportunities are not open to the private buyer, which means that to get on an even footing, the company may have to offer you much more than the 'cash equivalent' value for you to opt out of the company car market and buy yourself an acceptable replacement. It is often only when an employee is prepared to consider running an older car in place of the company one that he or she frees up some cash from the arrangement as well. For many employees, however, the stigma of going from a newish company car to an obviously second-hand one is too much to bear.

Special schemes

With the increasing interest in the principle of 'cash for cars', a number of motor manufacturers and leasing companies have come up with schemes which make the private purchase of a new car seem a more attractive proposition. In many ways these new 'low-cost' purchase plans are similar to traditional hire purchase but the monthly payments are much lower. To achieve this, you have to make a large lump sum payment – perhaps as much as a third or even half the new cost of the car – after three or four years when the scheme ends.

Low-cost purchase is also available to private car buyers and is covered in detail in Chapter 12. Many car dealers will be able to give you details for the type of car you are interested in buying, but you might also try talking to your company fleet manager, who is certain to have received details of such plans, and may be able to recommend one. If you want to replicate the sort of all-embracing cover that your company currently has for its fleet of cars, you can usually add cover for your routine repair and maintenance costs too.

BUYING YOUR COMPANY CAR

Businesses obtain their fleets of cars by one of two main methods. They either buy them outright from cash reserves they already hold, or they take them under contract hire. The fundamental difference is that contract-hired cars remain the property of the hire company. At the end of the agreed period – usually three or four years – they are returned and then sold off, often through car auctions, to the motor trade.

If you are interested in buying an ex-company car from your firm, it is worth making enquiries no matter what system is used

	Annual business mileage					
	up to 2,500		2,500 to 18,000		over 18,000	
	Income tax band					
	25%	40%	25%	40%	25%	40%
List price, on-the-road, incl extras	MONTHLY COST TO YOU (£)					
£ 5,000	36.46	58.33	24.30	38.89	12.15	19.44
£ 6,000	43.75	70.00	29.16	46.66	14.58	23.33
£ 7,000	51.04	81.67	34.02	54.44	17.01	27.22
£ 8,000	58.33	93.33	38.89	62.22	19.44	31.11
£ 9,000	65.63	105.00	43.75	69.99	21.87	35.00
£ 10,000	72.92	116.67	48.61	77.77	24.30	38.89
£ 11,000	80.21	128.33	53.47	85.55	26.73	42.77
£ 12,000	87.50	140.00	58.33	93.32	29.16	46.66
£ 13,000	94.79	151.67	63.19	101.10	31.59	50.55
£ 14,000	102.08	163.33	68.05	108.88	34.02	54.44
£ 15,000	109.38	175.00	72.91	116.66	36.45	58.33
£ 16,000	116.67	186.67	77.77	124.43	38.89	62.22
£ 17,000	123.96	198.33	82.63	132.21	41.32	66.10
£ 18,000	131.25	210.00	87.49	139.99	43.75	69.99
£ 19,000	138.54	221.67	92.35	147.76	46.18	73.88
£ 20,000	145.83	233.33	97.21	155.54	48.61	77.77
£ 21,000	153.13	245.00	102.07	163.32	51.04	81.66
£ 22,000	160.42	256.67	106.93	171.09	53.47	85.55
£ 23,000	167.71	268.33	111.79	178.87	55.90	89.44
£ 24,000	175.00	280.00	116.66	186.65	58.33	93.32
£ 25,000	182.29	291.67	121.52	194.43	60.76	97.21
£ 30,000	218.75	350.00	145.82	233.31	72.91	116.66
£ 35,000	255.21	408.33	170.12	272.20	85.06	136.10
£ 40,000	291.67	466.67	194.43	311.08	97.21	155.54
£ 45,000	328.13	525.00	218.73	349.97	109.36	174.98
£ 50,000	364.58	583.33	243.03	388.85	121.52	194.43

to run the fleet. Around 40 per cent of companies routinely sell cars to employees, and while in most cases these will have been cars owned by the company outright, many contract hire companies are prepared to do the same. The reason is that there are plenty of 3- to 4-year-old ex-company cars on the market, which means that the price obtained through an auction or as a trade-in is rarely particularly attractive. By selling to an employee the owner of the car can usually raise a much better price.

From your point of view buying an ex-company car can be a shrewd move. You probably know, or can find out, a fair deal about the car's history by talking to the user. And the price should still be very competitive, certainly nowhere near what a garage would charge, and often close to the 'trade' price. Ask whoever is responsible for the car fleet if you are interested in a particular car, even if you are not sure if your company operates such a policy.

THE REAL MONTHLY COST OF YOUR COMPANY CAR

The table on page 161 breaks down how much a company car will cost in terms of the reduced size of your monthly pay cheque.

CHAPTER 12

RAISING THE MONEY TO BUY YOUR CAR

The days when buying a car meant making a simple choice between cash or hire purchase are long gone. Now there are any number of ways to raise the finance, even if you have very little in the form of cash reserves of your own. One way or the other, most of us have to borrow when we come to replace our car, even a with another used one. It is very important to appreciate that the cost of borrowing the money varies just like the cost of buying the car. Depending upon who you choose to provide the loan, there will almost certainly be a big difference in the real cost in the long run. Put simply, it is quite easy to notch up fees and interest of £1,000 more than you need on a new car if you choose the 'wrong' source for your borrowing. So it is imperative to spend time first going through the options and then putting aside time to talk to everyone offering loans to make doubly sure that you end up with the best deal.

LOAN CONSIDERATIONS

When you are buying a car, there a number of obvious sources of money which will crop up again and again. Others, like an insurance loan, may be less familiar but could turn out to be the best option overall. Before going into the detail of loan types, however, it is important to consider a few key points which will apply to any loan you take out.

Security for the loan

The first point to understand is the difference between a *secured* and an *unsecured* loan. A secured loan is cheaper, but the lender – bank, building society, finance company or whatever – can take this security from you and sell it in order to recover the debt if you fail to meet the monthly payments. And as that security could be your home, it is not the type of loan to go for if there is the slightest risk that you may not be able to keep up the payments.

Unsecured loans have no such ties, but tend to be a little more expensive. The problem is, you may not be able to get one if you have fallen into arrears with a loan in the past and, anyway, they are not usually available if you want to borrow more than £10,000.

Monthly payments

Most loans are repaid on a monthly basis, so it is therefore possible to work out at the start how much you can afford to pay, and then see how big a loan that will finance. For secured loans, the payments are usually fixed over the whole period of borrowing the money. With unsecured loans, you might well find that the interest rate is variable, which means that your repayments could go up (or, less likely, down) over the course of the agreement.

With some types of loan, notably those arranged through the car dealer, you will be expected to make an initial down payment, or deposit. Typically, this will be between 20 per cent and 33 per cent of the car's value, but it could be more or less. Usually a dealer will be willing to take your car in part exchange as part or all of this down payment.

The length of the loan

The longer the period of the loan, the lower the monthly payments, but the more the car costs you in the long run. Generally, it is better to aim to pay off the loan in as short a period as you can comfortably handle, though you should ask the lender (better still, get it in writing) what would happen if you could not meet the monthly payments and wanted to extend the loan at a later date.

The cost of the loan

The Annual Percentage Rate (APR) lets you compare the real costs of borrowing, but does not tell the whole story. The APR is a useful benchmark, with the higher the APR figure you are quoted for the loan, the more expensive the credit. But APRs are difficult to compare when it comes to different types of credit.

Overdraft costs are very hard to compare, as the rate is based purely upon the interest and ignores any account charges on top. The APR on a personal loan does not include the cost of credit insurance, which can bump up the monthly payments considerably. Finally do not forget that interest rates for personal loans and hire purchase may be fixed at the outset, but on other forms of borrowing may not be.

Flexibility

Most types of loan have structured repayments so that you know how many payments you will have to make and when you have made the final one. Should you decide that you want to tidy up your affairs and repay a loan earlier than anticipated, you could well find that the lender is entitled to charge you a proportion of the extra interest and charges you would have paid if you had stuck with the loan for the full term. Check this out at the start if you feel early repayment is a possibility. If you borrow on an overdraft from your bank, there is much more flexibility – you can repay as soon as you wish.

Insurance

Many lenders will offer you some form of insurance against becoming unable to meet your regular monthly payments. Typically, the reasons for this might be illness, accident or unemployment. Naturally, there is an extra cost for this, against which you need to judge the risk involved of your needing this form of insurance. Whatever you do, check out the small print before you sign up, because there are often many restrictions built in which might make a particular policy unsuitable for you.

SOURCES OF LOANS

These days it seems possible to get loans without even getting out of bed – a telephone call will get at least the offer of a loan for a large number of people. The four popular sources are the bank, building society, car dealer and finance house. Banks and building societies work in much the same way, both offering personal loans of up to £10,000, usually unsecured. You can apply to any bank or building society for your loan, though with many you will need to open an ordinary account before they will give the all clear.

Virtually every car dealer will be able to offer you credit in the form of hire purchase (HP). This is not the dealer's cash, but comes either from a major finance company or from the car manufacturer's own loan sources. Hire purchase is a form of secured loan, in this case tied to the car; if you default, the car can be taken back.

Alternatively, you can go directly to one of the many finance houses advertising in the press. These loans are usually secured on your house, with many lenders offering you the chance to cut your monthly outgoings by spreading the repayments over as much as ten years.

As well as these common options for borrowing money to buy your car, there are a number of other alternatives. You might arrange an overdraft on your bank account, increase the mortgage on your house, or take out a loan on an insurance policy that you have had running for a number of years.

Pros and cons

Authorised overdraft

Going into the red on your current account.

For Flexible and convenient; can be cheap (check with your bank/building society); no security required.

Against Watch out for bank charges; bank can insist you pay it off at any time.

Gold Card overdraft

Cheap way of borrowing for people with gold cards.

For Cheaper than bank overdrafts; convenient and flexible; no security required.
Against Available only to people earning more than £20,000 a year; annual fee for the card could be over £80.

Personal loan

From banks, building societies, finance houses and some other lenders. You borrow for a set period and make set monthly repayments.
For Convenient; no security required (but see 'secured loans' below); usually no fees; potentially cheap, especially if borrowing for a couple of years.
Against Likely to be expensive to repay early; can't usually borrow for more than five years.

Secured loan

Like a personal loan, except that your home (or some other asset) is used as security for the loan.
For A cheap way of borrowing over the medium to long term, especially if the loan is from your mortgage lender and is added to your mortgage.
Against You could lose your home if you default on repayments; you may have to pay arrangement, valuation and legal fees; may be costly to repay early, particularly if you have borrowed over a long term.

Insurance policy loan

Offered against the surrender value of certain with-profits insurance policies.
For Cheap; you do not have to repay the loan until the policy matures.
Against Available only to people who have suitable policies which have been running for several years; still have to pay insurance premiums.

Hire purchase

The most common form of credit to be offered to car buyers by motor dealers.

For Very easy to arrange at the garage; interest rates can be extremely low.

Against Interest rates can also be higher than with other forms of borrowing; a sizeable deposit is usually required; you own the car only after all the credit has been repaid.

SPECIAL DEALS ON THE GARAGE FORECOURT

As well as the traditional form of car dealer credit – hire purchase – today's buyers are likely to be confronted with two new methods of financing their car purchase. Interest-free credit and 'low-cost purchase plans' have become extremely successful marketing tools, and though they are almost exclusively aimed at people buying brand-new cars, you can also find attractive finance deals on used cars.

Interest-free credit

Car manufacturers tend to run 'campaigns' lasting for a couple of months when they will offer interest-free credit on certain models in their range. If it is the type of car you are interested in buying, this can be an extremely attractive way of financing your purchase.

Interest-free credit on cars is not always quite as attractive as it first sounds, however. You may find that you are asked to put down a sizeable payment up front – perhaps as high as 50 per cent of the new cost of the car – in order to qualify for this deal. You might also find that the length of the interest-free credit period is very short – some schemes give you just a year to pay off the balance.

Finally, you must make sure that any interest-free, or low-cost, credit offered by the car dealer is not actually being surreptitiously financed by the price of the car. It's possible that the only way a dealer can offer the good finance deal is by cutting down on the discount he can give you – illegal, but it happens. So check with the salesman whether you could get a better deal by paying for cash and borrowing the money elsewhere.

The reverse is also true. Some salesmen get a sizeable kickback from their finance company if they sign up someone for premium-rate hire purchase, so may be able to offer you a lower price on the new car if you pay by hire purchase than if you paid by cash.

Low-cost purchase plans

Many motor manufacturers offer some form of 'low-cost' method of car finance. These generally start off in the same way as hire purchase: you make a down payment, or deposit, typically between 20 per cent and 40 per cent of the value of the car, followed by regular monthly payments. But these new low-cost schemes, with names such as 'Options', 'Choices', 'Select' and 'Solutions', are then rather different:

- the monthly payments are much lower than with traditional hire purchase
- you have to make a large lump sum payment at the end of the scheme. (With traditional hire purchase you normally have to make a nominal payment of a few pounds after the final monthly payment to take over full ownership of the car.)

The principle behind these low-cost schemes is that instead of paying for the whole value of the car over, say, three years, and then being left with a car which is still worth perhaps £5,000, you pay the difference between the initial cost and that £5,000. So after three years you still owe £5,000 and have to make a lump sum payment to complete the deal.

That is not nearly as bad as it first sounds. One option is to raise the money by selling the car. When you originally bought the car the final lump sum payment would have been carefully calculated so that, taking your predicted mileage into account, you should have no problem in realising that figure at sale time. Most people could hope to end up with some useful change in their pocket after they have made their final payment.

Option two is to use your car as part of the down payment for the next car you want to buy. If you owe £5,000, and a dealer is prepared to offer you £5,500 in part exchange for another car, that extra £500 can go towards your deposit. The final option, offered by almost all companies operating this type of deal, is the easiest of all. You hand back the car and the contract guarantees that this writes off any outstanding debt you have. The simplicity of this route, however, can be outweighed by the fact that the car you are handing back is worth significantly more than the debt you wish to offset. So always try to get an idea of what your car might be worth if you were instead to sell it privately, in order to avoid losing out financially.

You could, of course, take out a new loan, perhaps with a bank, to make that final payment and keep the car for longer. This could be a tempting route on a car you particularly like, though you might well find that it does not cost you a great deal more to take one of the above options and start on another scheme for a new car. You should also be aware that if you abuse your car before you have made your final payment – either by ill-treating it or driving more than the agreed annual mileage – it may not fetch the agreed final value, leaving you to find an additional sum to settle up.

Although the monthly payments will be much lower than with traditional hire purchase, and almost certainly any other form of borrowing, you still need to make sure that you are being charged a reasonable rate of interest. The advertising which cries out 'a new car for just £99 a month' may persuade you to visit the garage, but it will not be much good if you have to pay a huge deposit and high interest rates.

Example

The example opposite shows how the cost of traditional hire purchase compares with that of one of the new low-cost schemes. While the deposit is the same, the monthly payments are significantly reduced – from £465 to £289. The lower cost is also because Volkswagen, in common with many other car manufacturers, is promoting this type of car buying by offering more attractive interest rates.

The downside, of course, is that with the low-cost scheme you have to make a hefty final payment, in this case £6,450. This figure is the 'guaranteed residual value' should you decide at the end of the three-year period to return the car to the garage in lieu of the final payment. However, because this value would

Purchase of a Volkswagen Passat 2.0 GL over 3 years

	Traditional hire purchase	VW 'Solutions'	VW 'Solutions' with maintenance[1]
Cost new, 'on-the-road'	£17,089	£17,089	£17,089
Deposit/initial payment	£3,418	£3,418	£3,418
Followed by 35 monthly payments	£465	£289	£338
Followed by final payment	£465	£6,450	£6,450
Additional costs:			
Initial acceptance fee	£50	£50	£50
Final purchase fee	£10	£10	£10
Interest rate (APR) on finance	14.9%	10.2%	10.2%
Mileage limitation over three years	None	36,000	36,000
Cost for exceeded miles	None	3.5p/mile	3.5p/mile

[1] Maintenance includes the cost of services, repairs, tyres and road tax.

have been calculated at the outset based upon your estimated mileage, if you drive further than this, the second-hand value of the car will have been reduced. For that reason there is an 'excess mileage' clause, which is basically the amount the garage would charge you if you wanted to return the car.

Usually, you also have the option of combining the payment for the car with cover for all your routine costs, such as servicing, repairs and so on. You will probably find that the composition of the maintenance package can be adjusted to suit your needs, from merely taking the servicing option, to extending cover to tyres, repairs, breakdown service and other items. It is difficult to pass judgement on whether such arrangements are a sensible use of your resources. The companies offering such schemes have to take account of the risk of any very expensive repairs to your car, and so, like any form of mechanical breakdown insurance, the cost to you is likely to be higher than if you carried the risk yourself and just paid your way as and when it is required. But an all-in package will allow you to budget your monthly motoring expenditure very accurately.

FOUR DOS AND DON'TS IN BORROWING

DO Use the APR to compare the cost of borrowing, not the 'flat rate', which is misleading.

DO Consider the value of insurance cover for illness, accident and redundancy. It is usually offered, but not compulsory.

DO Check whether low-cost finance from the car dealer means that you cannot get such a good discount.

DO Look out for 'set-up charges', like £100 on a mortgage extension, £25 on a loan.

DON'T Borrow too much – it is very bad news if you fail to meet the payments.

DON'T Take out a fixed-term loan then expect to repay early; there could be hefty penalties.

DON'T Go for a variable interest rate loan when the bank interest rates are low – you could end up paying more later.

DON'T Get a loan secured on your house unless you are absolutely sure that, even in an emergency, you can find the money to meet all the payments.

CHAPTER 13

YOUR LEGAL RIGHTS

Buying and owning a car can give rise to a variety of problems. What are your rights if your new car is defective, and how do they differ if it is second-hand? Is buying from a car dealer safer than buying from a private seller? How do finance deals like hire purchase or credit sales affect your rights? What do you do if the car turns out to be stolen? What rights do you have when servicing or repairing a car or buying spare parts? How do you pursue a claim?

UNDERSTANDING THE LAW – A SHORT INTRODUCTION

Consumer protection comes from both **civil law** and **criminal law**. And within those areas the laws which protect you as a consumer are found in the form of **statutes** made by Parliament, and the **common law** decided by judges in cases argued out in the courts. But what do these terms mean?

- **Civil law** is the branch of the legal system which is of most use to the individual seeking compensation and redress. The civil law is concerned with rights and duties that relate to individuals in their dealings with other individuals (including companies and other groups of people). If you suffer loss because someone else breaches these laws then you have a right to redress and are entitled to take that person to court.

The main areas of civil law are **tort** (which includes negligence) and **contract**. The courts which deal with civil claims are the **county court** (which includes the **small claims court**) and the **High Court**.

- **Criminal law** is the branch of law which is concerned with offences against the public, and includes the Trade Descriptions Act 1968. Criminal law generally is enforced by the police, but the specific criminal law affecting consumers is enforced by public authorities like Trading Standards Departments and Environmental Health Officers (both at your local council offices). You cannot get compensation directly by reporting a criminal offence such as a false trade description, but a criminal prosecution will give added weight to your civil complaint. The courts which deal with criminal matters are the **magistrates courts** and the **Crown Courts**.
- **Statute law** is set down in Acts of Parliament (such as the Sale of Goods Act 1979) and in Regulations and Orders made under the general authority of Acts of Parliament. These set out the rights and duties of specified people, in specified circumstances.
- **Common law** is based on the decisions of the courts in actual cases which also set out the rights and duties of people in different circumstances. These are recorded in law reports and form 'precedents' for the future. In this way the courts can adapt the law to new situations without having to wait for Parliament to introduce statutes. And many cases that come before the courts are interpreting and defining the words in various Acts of Parliament.

THE FIVE MAJOR STATUTES WHICH PROTECT YOU

The **statutes** which protect you as a car owner cover areas of civil and criminal law. There are five major statutes to note:

1 **Sale of Goods Act 1979** offers protection when buying goods, a car or spare parts, say. This is perhaps the most important single piece of consumer legislation. It sets down the obligations

on business when selling goods to consumers. Whatever the contract of sale says, and whether written or spoken, the Sale of Goods Act 1979 implies terms into that contract (see page 180). It says that when you buy goods from a trader (whether they are new, second-hand, or in a 'sale') those goods must:

- belong to the person selling them
- fit any **description** given of them
- be of **merchantable quality**
- be reasonably **fit for their purpose**
- correspond with any **sample** you were shown.

2 **Supply of Goods and Services Act 1982** offers protection when using the services of a trader to service or repair your car, for example. Contracts where the trader provides not merely goods such as spare parts, or materials for repairing something, but also the labour element, are classified in law as contracts for **work and materials**. When you ask somebody to carry out a service for you, this Act defines the standard of the service you can legally expect, the quality of the materials used, and gives guidance on other elements such as price and time for performance. The Act imposes the following legal duty on the supplier of the service (although this statute does not apply in Scotland, the common law gives similar rights):

- to carry out the service with reasonable skill and care
- to carry out the service within a 'reasonable time' where no time limit has been fixed
- to make a 'reasonable charge' for the service where no charge has been agreed in advance
- to use materials which are of merchantable quality and fit for their purpose – these have the same meaning as under the Sale of Goods Act 1979.

3 **Consumer Protection Act 1987 and, in Northern Ireland, the (N.I.) Order 1987** Briefly, this states that manufacturers are strictly liable if the products they make are defective and cause personal injury, or damage to your property over £275, and allows you to claim compensation. It also makes it a criminal offence for traders to give price indications and make bargain

offers which are misleading. The crucial provisions for getting compensation are that:

- you have to prove that the product was **defective** and that it **caused** the injury or damage that you are complaining of
- a product is considered **defective** if it is **less safe** than consumers generally are entitled to expect, so the goods must be unsafe, not merely shoddy. A car could therefore be defective under this Act if the instructions for use or any warnings are inadequate, making it unsafe to use
- it does not take away the existing liability of retailers under the Sale of Goods Act 1979
- it applies to products **supplied** after March 1988
- you cannot claim for damage to the product itself. So if your car breaks down completely but does not damage you or anything else, say, this law will not help you, although you may be able to claim against the retailer for this sort of damage under the contract of sale.

4 **Consumer Credit Act 1974** offers protection when making credit agreements and, in some circumstances, gives you the right to claim against the finance company if the retailer or supplier of defective goods or services goes bust. It regulates credit agreements and gives purchasers a number of rights: advertisements for credit schemes must show true rates of interest without hidden extras; purchasers have certain rights to pay off the debt earlier than the time for payment laid down in the agreement; if purchasers sign a credit agreement at home, there is a cooling-off period during which they are allowed to change their mind and cancel the agreement; when making credit agreements the Act sets out formalities which the dealer and finance company must comply with – these ensure you are given the best information and copies of the contract. It is also a criminal offence to supply any kind of credit without being licensed by the Office of Fair Trading (see Addresses).

5 **Misrepresentation Act 1967 and, in Northern Ireland, the Misrepresentation Act (N.I.) 1967** If purchasers enter an agreement on the basis of a statement purporting to be a fact but

which turns out to be untrue, they have the right to cancel the deal and get their money back if they act quickly, or to compensation. This applies equally to trade and private sales. The Act does not apply to Scotland, although the law there is broadly similar.

Three other statutes are worthy of note:

- **Hire Purchase Act 1964, Part III** When you buy goods on HP you do not legally own them until the final instalment has been paid. Until then they belong to the HP company and are **hired** to you. If you want to sell the goods before the final instalment has been paid, you have to tell the HP company and pay off what you owe. The general rule is that you will have to hand the goods back to the finance company, which remains the real owner. However, this Act says that where a person sells a **vehicle** which is on HP to a **private purchaser** who does not know about the outstanding HP agreement, the buyer becomes the legal owner. The HP company would have to sue the seller and has no right to recover the vehicle from the innocent private buyer.
- **Unfair Contract Terms Act 1977** The small print in contracts for the sale of goods can never take away purchasers' rights under the Sale of Goods Act. Other notices or conditions in contracts which exclude or restrict liability for financial loss or damage to property have to be fair and reasonable. If they are not, they will be invalid under the Act and will not affect a claim.
- **Trade Descriptions Act 1968** This makes it a criminal offence for traders to make false statements about the goods or any connected services they sell. This covers many things concerning the physical characteristics of the goods and their history – for example, statements about quantity, size and performance, as well as statements about who the item was manufactured by and where, and previous ownership. False descriptions about motor vehicles and accessories make up the biggest number of convictions under this Act. Report any problems to the local Trading Standards Department (see Addresses).

BUYING A CAR

Making a contract (verbal and written)

Your contract with the seller gives you your rights. Contracts for hire-purchase and other credit transactions *must* be in writing, but this is an exception and not the rule. Generally contracts do not have to be, and every day we make contracts without putting them in writing, and even without a single word being spoken – we buy food in shops, pay taxi or bus fares, for example. All these have the same standing as written contracts, and are governed by the same laws. So, whether written or verbal, a contract is an agreement that can be enforced by the law and gives rise to rights and responsibilities for those involved.

Spoken agreements can cause problems as it may be difficult to prove the precise terms agreed, such as the price, or a delivery date. If you do not have a proper written contract keep any evidence you do have; for example, keep receipts or invoices in case you need to prove later where you bought the goods and how much you paid.

A contract will usually include **implied** terms and **express** terms. Whether written or verbal, some rights are always implied into certain transactions by Acts of Parliament – like the Sale of Goods Act 1979 when you buy goods – and these rights can *never* be taken away (see page 179). Other things expressly agreed between you and the seller are express terms, like price, colour, extras, and so on.

It is important to remember that if you sign a contract (usually with lots of small print on the back), you will normally be bound by it whether you have read it or not, and the terms of a written agreement will almost always override anything that you have agreed verbally. So, take time to read everything before signing. If you do sign, even if you did not see the full terms because they were contained in a separate document and you did not request to see a copy, as long as you were referred to that document (for example, 'full terms and conditions available on request') you will probably be bound by them. It is up to you to check them out. You can still challenge some of the small print, but you may have to go to court to do so.

The seller should stick to express terms such as the colour, date of delivery, the price, and any extras to be included. If, for example, the seller tries to increase the price to take into account increases in the manufacturer's prices, look carefully at your sales agreement. If this says it can, you will have to pay. If it does not, you are not obliged to pay. So check any contract before signing. If there is a term which lets the seller increase the price, strike it out before you sign and ask the seller to agree to the amendments you have made.

If you cancel the order, you have broken the contract, as ultimately you should have taken delivery and paid the balance of the price. In most cases a deposit is taken as security to make the buyer have second thoughts before attempting to cancel the contract, so the seller is entitled to keep the deposit. In addition, the seller may be entitled to claim from you any loss of profit over and above the amount of the deposit – for example, if a car had been specially adapted for you to a precise specification which would not be easy to sell to anyone else. Fortunately, most cars are of a standard design and specification and dealers do not have problems selling them on to recover their loss, so you should only lose the deposit, although you cannot bank on it.

The following are points to watch out for:

- *never* sign a document until you have read it. *If in doubt, do not sign,* and ask to take it away to think about it. Thinking time is your right
- if you are not happy with some of the terms, cross them out and ask for the agreement to be retyped, or make sure your amendments are signed by the company representative
- *always* ask for a copy of the final agreement carrying both your signature and that of the other person
- if the small print in contracts for goods or services attempts to take away or limit your rights to claim under the Sale of Goods Act 1979, this is illegal, your statutory rights cannot be taken away. Report this to the local Trading Standards Department (see Addresses)

- other notices or conditions in contracts which try to take away or restrict your rights must be fair and reasonable. If they are not, they will be invalid under the Unfair Contract Terms Act 1977 and can be ignored
- if defective goods or workmanship cause death or personal injury, your right to claim compensation can *never* be taken away by a notice or contract term
- look for a trade association sign – this should ensure that the dealer complies with the motor industry Code of Practice and also means you can seek help from the association if things go wrong (see page 211).

What are your rights?

Whatever the contract of sale says, and whether written or spoken, the **Sale of Goods Act 1979** implies terms into that contract. It says that when you buy goods from a trader (whether they are new, second-hand or in a 'sale') those goods must:

- belong to the person selling them – if the seller does not have **title** to the goods (i.e. own them) then you will not normally become the owner, even after paying your money
- fit any **description** given of them – whether this was in a brochure, stated by the dealer in an advertisement, or otherwise. So if you were told the car was fitted with an airbag and ABS brakes it must fit that description
- be of **merchantable quality** – so they must be in good condition and free of faults, and able to do the job expected of them (taking into account their price, age and so on)
- be reasonably **fit for their purpose** – so if you told the seller you needed them for a specific purpose (for example, towing a caravan) then they should be fit for that purpose as well as withstanding general use
- correspond with any **sample** you were shown – so if you place an order on the basis of a sample of the goods (material for the paintwork or interior trim, for example), the finished goods must correspond with that sample.

Who are your rights against?

If the goods do not meet any of these requirements, it is the retailer (rather than the manufacturer) who is in breach of the contract of sale and is thus under a legal obligation to sort out your problem. If goods are not up to scratch, the law allows you either to **reject** them and claim your money back, plus compensation for any extra loss suffered, or claim **compensation**, usually the cost of repair, plus any extra loss suffered.

Your right to **reject** the goods and get your **money back** can be lost with the passage of time, regardless of whether you could have known about the defect before it came to light. You lose the right to reject faulty goods once you have 'accepted' them. The Sale of Goods Act says that you have 'accepted' the goods where you keep them for a 'reasonable' time before rejecting them. There is no precise legal definition of 'reasonable' – it depends on the circumstances of each case – but it is a matter of a few weeks, maybe days. As it stands, the law is extremely prejudicial to consumers. The problem with complex goods like cars is that time may have run out before you discover the fault. If you are too late to reject, you still have the other remedy: the right to **compensation**. So the seller ought to pay the full cost of repairing the car plus any other expenses arising from the breach (cost of hire cars, etc.). Some car dealers now offer a refund or replacement as a matter of goodwill. Also check any guarantee to see if a refund is promised.

In one well-known case the High Court decided that it was too late for a consumer to reject a new car after only three weeks and 142 miles, even though a defect, which caused the engine to seize up, could not have been discovered earlier. Although he could not get his money back, the buyer was fully compensated for the **cost of repair**, plus compensation for the hassle caused on the day the car broke down. Even so, he was stuck with a repaired car.

It also does not matter whether the seller knows the car is defective or not, even if it worked when it was sold to you. The Sale of Goods Act 1979 imposes '**strict liability**' on retailers. This means that the goods they sell must satisfy each of the various implied terms, including the merchantable quality condition. If they do not, they will be liable for **breach of contract**. It is no defence for the seller to show that he or she did not know, and could not reasonably be expected to have discovered the fault. So, although the fault may have been caused by the wiring or a defective microchip which could not possibly have been noticed, the seller is still fully responsible because of the contract with the customer. And if the seller tells you to claim on your manufacturer's guarantee, do not be put off by this – you do not have to do it. A retailer may throw in its own 'warranty' free with the car. This may offer, for example, free membership of one of the breakdown services, or free windscreen replacement. Such promises become part of the contract of sale (express terms) and you can insist that these services are provided if you need them or claim the cost if the retailer refuses.

The price

By law, unless the price is clearly shown as excluding VAT, the price you are given includes VAT, so you cannot be charged extra later. The same goes for non-optional extras. If these are charged separately, then the seller must make it clear whether the price is inclusive or exclusive. And any compulsory extra costs (delivery charges, registration plates and tax, for example) must be displayed as prominently as the main price in retailers' ads and showroom displays. It is an offence not to, so report any problems to the local Trading Standards Department (see Addresses).

If you order a new car and do agree a total price, the garage cannot charge you extra because of a mistake in its original calculations. By agreeing a fixed price with the garage, a contract is made and you can insist on getting the car for that sum. As long as the mistake was unknown to you the car should be yours for the agreed price.

If the garage refuses to let you have the car at the agreed price, you should give it a written time limit of seven days, say, to deliver the vehicle. If it does not, you can buy the same model somewhere else as cheaply as possible, and, if the price is higher, claim the additional sum from the garage.

The same applies if, when buying a car, the manufacturer's recommended price rises between the time you place the order and the time of delivery. Always check the contract of sale as it may allow the garage to pass on price rises to you.

Delivery delays

If you order a car, you may be given a delivery period – 10–12 weeks, say. Many car dealers' standard terms also state that 'time for delivery is not of the essence of the contract'. If you do not make known any special reasons why the delivery date is vitally important to you, and if the company does not meet the delivery date, you cannot cancel the contract:

- if the goods are not delivered within a 'reasonable' time, you can get around any further delays. You should write giving the company reasonable notice and imposing a deadline – if the car was not supplied within one week at the latest, say, you would treat the contract as at an end
- unless you have made time of the essence, in the absence of a notice imposing a strict time-limit in that way, you are legally obliged to continue with the contract and let the company deliver the car
- assuming the car is in fact ready for delivery the following week and you refuse to accept delivery, you would find yourself saddled with considerable expense, as the car may have been specially ordered for you. However, if it is likely that it could be sold to another customer, you would not be liable for the total contract price.

What about minor defects?

If you notice a scratch on the side of your newly delivered car, whether you can complain depends on how bad the scratch is. If it is bad enough to affect the look of the item or the way the goods work, you may be able to argue that it is not of merchantable quality. However, there is a basic legal principle which says that the law does not concern itself with very minor matters. So if the scratch is a **minor defect** and very small, this will not give rise to a legal claim to reject it.

Part exchange

With such a deal your rights are exactly the same as if you had paid in full for the new car. You have the full protection of the Sale of Goods Act 1979. Make sure that the price you are paying and the value you are getting are written down. Look in the *Which? Guide to New and Used Cars* to check the value of the car you are trading-in so you get a good deal. Although this is not as convenient as a part-exchange deal, you may get more for your old car by selling it separately.

Second-hand cars from dealers

If you buy a second-hand car from a trader (even if you sign a form which said 'sold as seen') the Sale of Goods Act 1979 applies, so it must fit the **description**, be of **merchantable quality**, and be **fit for its purpose** (see page 180). To prevent any hassle later, get the car checked over by the AA, RAC or any other independent expert, before you buy. Obviously, a second-hand car will not be in such good condition as a new car, but it should be roadworthy, and the quality you can expect will depend on the age, the price and the description given of the car:

- you may need an engineer's report to show that the car was defective at the time you purchased it, was not of merchantable quality or as described. You may also argue that there was a **misrepresentation** which led you to buy the car
- if you act quickly enough, you are entitled to reject the car and get your money back (see page 181). If you have lost the right to reject, or if you want to keep the car, you are entitled to compensation for the defective engine, which is usually taken to be the cost of a repair.

Second-hand cars and 'clocking'

The supply of second-hand cars where the mileometer (odometer) has been changed is a major problem (see Chapter 2). It is an offence (a breach of the Trade Descriptions Act 1968 – see page 177) if the recorded mileage is not correct. A buyer is likely to assume that the odometer reading is an indication of the true mileage of the vehicle. Some unscrupulous car dealers attempt to avoid committing an offence by attaching a sticker to the odometer which says that the indication is, or may be, incorrect. But to escape liability the disclaimer must be adequate – bold, precise and clearly displayed before the sale is made. If it becomes clear that the trader has deliberately zeroed or clocked the odometer then no disclaimer can help him to avoid liability. The motor industry Code of Practice sets out guidelines for its members. These state that they must:

- take reasonable steps to verify the recorded mileage of a used car and try to get a signed statement from the previous owner
- unless the dealer is satisfied with the accuracy of the quoted mileage, he should not quote the mileage in adverts, negotiations, etc.

You can also take steps to protect yourself by asking to see the vehicle registration document before buying, take a note of the previous keeper and check out the mileage by contacting him or her. Cars older than three years must have an MOT certificate (see Chapter 5). Ask to see this too: it shows the mileage at the time of the last test.

If you purchase a car with a false odometer reading, and if there was no indication (a sticker, for example) warning you that the odometer may be wrong, there are two courses open to you:

- you may pursue your rights in civil law under the Sale of Goods Act 1979 (misdescription) – see page 174 – or under the Misrepresentation Act 1967 (misrepresentation) – see page 176
- secondly, you should report the matter to your local Trading Standards Department. The Trade Descriptions Act 1968 makes it a criminal offence for dealers to make false statements about the cars they sell. Since it is criminal law, the Act cannot help you directly if you want to make a claim for compensation, but if the trading standards officer does decide to prosecute you may ask the court for compensation. It is worth threatening that you will report the matter as it may lead to a quick settlement of your case.

Buying second-hand cars privately

Private ads in local papers often give a description of the car on sale. When you buy goods from a **private seller** the principle of 'caveat emptor' ('let the buyer beware') applies. There is no legal requirement that the goods are of merchantable quality or fit for their purpose. With private sales you will only have redress if:

- the goods do not correspond with any **description** you have been given, or
- the seller was guilty of **misrepresentation**, or
- the seller does not really own the goods (see page 189).

So, if a car is merely described as a Ford Mondeo 1.6, with 16,000 miles on the clock, then as long as it is a 1.6 Mondeo with 16,000 on the clock you may be unable to do anything if it breaks down. However, if the car is described as being as good as new and regularly serviced, for example, and this is clearly not true, there will be two possible claims:

- **breach of description** This entitles you to reject the car and get your money back, or keep it and ask for compensation (usually the cost of repair – see page 181 for loss of right to reject)
- **misrepresentation** This entitles you to cancel the contract and get your money back, or keep it and ask for compensation. A misrepresentation is a statement of fact (not opinion) which is made by the seller before the contract is made. If you relied on that statement when deciding whether to buy and it turns out to be wrong, you can claim, even if the statement was not deliberately wrong.

In any dispute with the seller where there has been a written or verbal statement about the car it is probably best to allege both a breach of contract and misrepresentation.

You can try to protect yourself when buying a second-hand car. As your legal rights are limited it is almost impossible to protect yourself fully against hidden defects and legal problems. However, here are a few tips which should help (see also Chapter 2):

- employ an engineer to check the car over and report on the car's condition. This is especially important if you are buying from a private seller. If you are a member of a motoring organisation it may provide a vehicle inspection report if requested
- carry out a search with HP Information plc (HPI) – see Addresses. You can apply to HPI direct and you will be charged a fee for each search. An HPI search does not guarantee that the car you buy is OK but it will tell you whether the car is recorded as:
  being subject to an outstanding finance agreement
  having had a major damage-related insurance claim
  stolen or at risk from theft or fraud
  having been subject to a registration plate change
- try and make a note of everything that the seller says about the car – it would be useful to take an independent witness along with you so that you have proof that any claims made were really said. Also, hang on to the advert if it contains a description of the car
- read the latest *Which?* report on buying a second-hand car – following the advice should help you avoid costly mistakes.

Buying at auction

Although the Sale of Goods Act 1979 applies, the main legal rules can be excluded by a notice on display or in the catalogue – so beware, and check the auction house conditions before you bid. Auctions are a popular place to buy many types of goods, most commonly cars (see Chapter 1). If you buy at an auction, your rights are against the seller, who could prove difficult to trace and, unlike in an ordinary consumer transaction where your statutory rights cannot be excluded, your rights at an auction may be limited, so you will have little or no redress if the goods are faulty. So buy only if you are satisfied about the condition of the car – you may know what to look for, or get the car checked over by an expert first.

Manufacturers' guarantees

These may be offered free when you buy a car, or at an extra cost for an 'extended warranty'. Many manufacturers promise to repair faults free of charge. Some offer your money back, others offer a replacement. Always check the wording of a guarantee to see what is included.

The important things to remember about free guarantees are as follows:

- these are **in addition to your rights** against the seller under the Sale of Goods Act 1979 and are not in any way an alternative to those rights. The manufacturer is legally obliged to explain this to you and you should see the words 'This does not affect your statutory rights'. In fact it is a criminal offence to try to limit a consumer's Sale of Goods Act rights. The retailer may say that you cannot complain if the product goes wrong after the manufacturer's guarantee has expired. So, if the exhaust system gives up the day after the manufacturer's one-year exhaust warranty expires, do not worry. An exhaust on a new car should last longer than this so you should still insist the retailer puts it right – the car is clearly not of merchantable quality (see page 180)
- there is some doubt whether such a free manufacturer's guarantee is legally enforceable in England and Wales (in Scotland it is enforceable because Scots law treats such guarantees as contracts between the consumer and the manufacturer)
- in practice most manufacturers honour their guarantees anyway
- the fact that the guarantee lasts only for one year may give the impression that this is the only period of durability which you are entitled to expect. In fact the extent of the cover offered by the manufacturer has no effect on your statutory rights against the seller
- as manufacturers are under no legal obligation to offer guarantees they may make them as limited in scope as they wish, and often do.

While there may be doubt about the legal status of free guarantees, you can pursue your rights under an extended warranty for which you have paid. By paying for the warranty you have made a contract with the manufacturer. In practice, many people will automatically claim against the manufacturer under any guarantee or warranty they have. The motor industry Code of Practice says what manufacturers should do when it comes to claims under warranty – check with the Society of Motor Manufacturers and Traders (SMMT – see Addresses). But always consider first whether your rights are better against the retailer. Most warranties are peppered with terms which define and limit the liability of the manufacturer – for example, you may have to pay for the labour while the parts are supplied free. It is worth approaching the retailer first about the problem. It may agree that the manufacturer should do the work under warranty – but tell the seller that it should pay for any extra costs involved (the labour charge or alternative hire car charges, say). Whoever repairs your faulty car, you should not be left out of pocket.

IS THE SELLER ENTITLED TO SELL THE CAR?

Astonishingly, there is no totally reliable way of proving who owns a car. You cannot rely on the registration documents: they only show the 'registered keeper', who may not be the owner (the car may, for example, be a company car). The Hire Purchase Information plc (HPI) scheme, though a good idea, is not a 100 per cent guarantee. There are a number of reasons why you may find a disgruntled company or individual claiming back the car you had bought in good faith from someone else.

Stolen goods

If you buy a car that turns out to be stolen, in nearly all cases you have no right to keep it. The car may have been stolen some time before you bought it. The seller may know nothing about this either. But somewhere there will be the original owner who wants the car back. It is a very complicated area. The Sale of Goods Act

1979 says that a person who sells goods (whether a dealer or private seller) must be the real owner (have title), or have the consent of the real owner to sell. If your seller had no right to sell the car, as he or she was not the owner and not in a position to transfer the ownership to you, the original owner from whom the car was stolen remained the real owner throughout. If you refuse to return the car, the original owner will be able to bring a civil action in the courts for what lawyers call 'conversion'. The court may order you to pay the value of the car at the date you bought it, or, more likely, order you to return the car.

Even if this happens, all is not lost:

- you may recover the full price from your seller. The reason is that under the Sale of Goods Act 1979 the requirement that a seller must own the goods he or she sells means that your seller is in breach of his contract with you. So you are entitled to a full refund. It is irrelevant that your seller was completely innocent and had no knowledge or suspicion that the car was stolen – like most of the obligation under the Act, it is a 'strict liability' on the seller
- it is equally irrelevant that your seller was a private seller, as the provision as to title applies to private and trade sales alike
- there is one odd legal provision which may help you to keep the car, called **market overt**. This quirky exception to the general rule is full of complicated points – for instance, it applies if, before it reached your seller, the car had been previously sold in a market or fair established by charter or custom, and the sale took place between sunrise and sunset. It is not quite as odd as it sounds. Many car thieves find markets and fairs ideal places to get rid of stolen goods, so it is worth investigating the history of the car since it was stolen to establish whether the car is really yours to keep.

If you improved the car before you realised it was stolen, the Torts (Interference with Goods) Act 1977 says that you are entitled to receive compensation for the repairs and improvements you make. This Act can be used like a shield, not a sword, so if the true owner of the car takes you to court to get the car back, the court will make an allowance for the increase in value of the car which is attributable to the repairs and improvements you make. Your position will be much weaker if you let the true owner take the car back without going to court, because then you cannot use this Act as a sword to claim your expenses back from the true owner. So while there is a dispute, it is best to park the car on your property if possible, and do not give anyone permission to take it away. Try to negotiate a reasonable payment and avoid going to court if you can. But if a court does order you to hand the car over, you should be able to recover the full purchase price from the person who sold the car to you (see above).

Car still owned by a finance company

You probably think that when you buy a car you automatically become the legal owner. If you buy the car from someone who has an unpaid loan outstanding for it, you do become the owner. With most credit deals the debtor borrows money to buy the goods and any dispute about unpaid instalments is between the finance company (creditor) and the borrower – it has no effect on the subsequent ownership of the goods. But this is not always the case.

When buying a car (or any goods) on HP, the 'buyer' does not legally own it until the final instalment has been paid. Until then it belongs to the HP company and is merely **hired** to him. If he wants to sell it before the final instalment has been paid, he has to tell the HP company and pay off what is owed. Unless the buyer does so, the car continues to belong to the HP company and your 'purchase' of it does not make you the owner, although you could recover your money from the 'seller', assuming you can still find that person. So, if the second-hand car you buy turns out to be still on hire purchase, the finance company may want to reclaim the car. Under an HP agreement the goods are still owned by the finance company until the hirer has paid all that was due under the HP agreement. So until then he has nothing more than a right to possession of the car and has no right to sell it.

The Hire Purchase Act 1964 offers protection specifically where a **motor vehicle** which is the subject of an outstanding

HP agreement is sold to a **private purchaser**. Provided you (the private purchaser) did not know about the existence of the outstanding hire-purchase agreement, or you were even told about it but informed it had been paid off, you will obtain a good title to the vehicle and be able to resist the finance company's claims. So if you meet these criteria the car is legally yours to keep. The finance company will have to fight it out with the dishonest seller (this does not apply in Northern Ireland).

Illogically, this protection does not apply to cars which are let out under a leasing agreement, even though this sort of agreement has much in common with an HP agreement. The main difference is that under an HP agreement, the hirer has a **right** to buy the car; under a leasing agreement, he has not.

DANGEROUS VEHICLES AND PRODUCT LIABILITY

Harsh as it may sometimes seem, the retailer is legally responsible for the quality of products sold: we have seen they must be of 'merchantable quality', fit for their purpose and comply with any description given. The retailer must also fulfil any express terms of the contract of sale. This is a strict liability, so, even if it did not know of the problem your rights are still against the retailer. Where goods are faulty in themselves it is not the manufacturer's responsibility. Product liability does not help you when goods are merely shoddy or break down. You should go back to the shop and exercise your rights as a buyer under the Sale of Goods Act 1979.

Check to see whether you received a manufacturer's guarantee when you bought the vehicle. If the guarantee has not expired, the manufacturer may put things right under the terms of the guarantee cover. Otherwise, the manufacturer will only be liable if:

- the fault was such as to make the vehicle **unsafe** and you actually suffered some damage to yourself or your property (other than the car itself) as a result of this.

The term 'product liability' is therefore a confusing one as in law it is generally used to describe the legal position between a consumer and the manufacturer. This is to distinguish it from the legal relationship between a consumer and the retailer where your rights are governed by contract law. But you do not have a contract with the manufacturer. So, a different set of legal principles apply if you want to hold the manufacturer responsible for losses you suffer because of a problem with the product. Product liability laws are usually relied on when the product in question has proved to be unsafe in some way and has either caused physical injury or damage to other property.

The Consumer Protection Act 1987 makes manufacturers 'strictly liable' for 'defective' products where that defect caused death or injury, or damage to property other that the defective product itself. It is designed to give **all** users of goods (and not just those who happened to buy them, as under the Sale of Goods Act) the right to claim against the manufacturer for compensation for injury or damage you suffer as a direct result of the lack of safety in the car. Damage to property must amount to at least £275 (a purely arbitrary figure designed to prevent lots of minor claims against manufacturers), but even minor personal injury is covered.

'Defect' here does not mean that the car merely breaks down (for that you will have to claim against the seller if you can); it means **less safe** than consumers generally are entitled to expect, so the goods must be unsafe, not merely shoddy. A car could therefore be defective under this Act if the instructions for use or any warnings are inadequate, making it unsafe to use.

If you did not buy the car yourself (it was a present, say) you have no contract with the seller and so cannot claim under the Sale of Goods Act 1979. So any claim will be against the manufacturer under the Consumer Protection Act 1987. This does not allow you to claim for damage to the car itself but does allow you to claim for the damage to anything else (your garage or house, say) and any injury to you. If you were injured, you will need medical evidence from your GP or a specialist. You may also be covered for the damage to the building and contents under your household insurance, so check this carefully.

It is the manufacturer's responsibility to fit safety features to its products. If you suffer damage or injury because a manufacturer has ignored current safety measures, for example, if you suffer severe head injuries which could have been prevented if an airbag had been fitted on the steering wheel, you may be able to claim compensation. You could argue that the failure to fit an airbag means that the car is less safe than consumers are reasonably entitled to expect. So, much will depend on when the car was manufactured. In any claim where you have been seriously injured, you should seek the advice of a specialist personal injury solicitor. Contact the Law Society or the Association of Personal Injury Lawyers (see Addresses).

Unroadworthy vehicles

It is a criminal offence to sell a motor vehicle in an 'unroadworthy condition'. This means cars which do not comply with regulations as to brakes, steering gear, tyres or construction generally, or where the condition of the vehicle poses a danger of injury to anybody if it is used on a road. A criminal prosecution here does not mean you will automatically get compensation, but if a car you have bought is unroadworthy the seller may be liable to you for compensation (either a refund or a repair – see page 181) under the Sale of Goods Act 1979. Report any problems to the local Trading Standards Department (see Addresses).

Product recalls

There is no law that manufacturers must take positive action to recall vehicles if a design or manufacturing defect is discovered. They may be at fault if they know of a defect but do not recall, and they may also be liable for the injuries and damage caused to consumers if the product is unsafe – so they may have to pay out compensation in individual cases. But the law does not presently recognise that prevention is better than cure.

If your vehicle is the subject of a recall it makes it much easier to prove that there was a defect. The evidence has, in a way, been provided by the manufacturer – it will be difficult for it to argue that the product was not defective if the fault that caused your car to burst into flames and burn down your garage, say, is the same as the one that prompted the recall. It may be advisable to have the product in question examined by an appropriate independent expert to confirm what the nature of the problem was. The manufacturer will probably also be more keen to sort out problems when there has already been the bad publicity of a recall.

Product recalls are usually advertised in the national press, and *Which?* magazine carries details of them every month. If you have such a product, you should contact the manufacturer immediately. If it is already too late and the damage is done, then you should still get in touch with the manufacturer and ask it for compensation.

There are few guidelines for domestic product recalls. No one can force a manufacturer to initiate a product recall although the government can make a manufacturer issue a notice warning people about an unsafe product. This is usually enough of a threat to make most manufacturers institute a recall. Some products, like medicines and foods, have special rules to make sure unsafe products get taken off the market as soon as possible but not, unfortunately, motor vehicles.

REPAIRS AND SERVICING YOUR CAR

If work done by a repairer fails, or a new part installed by the garage breaks down, say, you do not have to pay to have the problem put right. And it does not matter if the parts supplied by the garage broke down because of a manufacturing fault – the garage should supply parts that are of merchantable quality and fit for their purpose under the Supply of Goods and Services Act 1982 (common law in Scotland). It is no defence for the garage to say that the staff were careful and had no reason to suspect that the part was defective. The garage should not charge you for putting the car right, and should provide the parts and labour free of charge. If not, you are entitled to have the work done elsewhere and ask the garage to pay the bill plus any extra expense, such as car hire while your car is off the road.

The Supply of Goods and Services Act 1982 (common law in Scotland) also states that the work should be done with reasonable care and skill. As a garage is under a duty to carry out repairs carefully, it is responsible for any incompetent and careless work of the mechanics. There is a possibility that you could have signed away your right to compensation if you signed a contract and it had a clause excluding the garage's liability for negligence. This clause must be reasonable, and if it is not, it will have no effect on your rights (see below).

Ideally, you would be entitled to take the car back and ask the garage to put things right free of charge. But if you have really lost confidence in the repairer, and do not trust the garage to do the job properly, you can have the problems put right by someone else and charge the cost to the original repairer. If the car is beyond repair, you should be entitled to compensation – this would be the difference between the value of the car before the damage and in its condition after plus a refund of the wasted repair charges. Many garages are members of one of the **trade associations** such as the Retail Motor Industry Federation (RMI) and the Scottish Motor Trade Association (SMTA) – see Addresses – which adhere to the **motor industry Code of Practice**. If the dealer is a member and you are having difficulty getting a problem sorted out, tell the relevant association about your complaint as soon as possible. It may be able to resolve the problem. If that does not work, you have the choice of going to court or taking your claim to arbitration (see page 210).

Services – exclusions

If you pick up your car from the repairer and discover damage, complain immediately (so there is no chance for anyone to accuse you of causing it yourself). Do not be put off by signs saying: 'We cannot accept responsibility for the loss of or damage to goods howsoever caused.' The Supply of Goods and Services Act 1982 entitles you to have the repairs carried out with reasonable care and skill, and if not, you are entitled to claim compensation. However, it is very common in business contracts, particularly contracts for services, to find terms which attempt to limit or exclude liability for a variety of things. These are commonly called **exclusion** or **exemption clauses**. The Unfair Contract Terms Act 1977 regulates these and allows suppliers to hide behind them even if they have been negligent, so long as the clause is **fair and reasonable**. What is fair and reasonable depends on the circumstances of each case. Such factors that may be taken into account are the bargaining position of both you and the garage, whether you could have got the service elsewhere on different terms, or had you ever used that garage before. It is very unlikely that a court would allow a garage to rely on a notice which tried to exempt them for all responsibility for loss and damage, whatever the cause. So do not be put off pursuing such a claim just because of the sign. Each case depends on the individual facts.

When you take your car into a garage for repairs, the garage must take reasonable care of it. If your car is damaged while in the possession of the garage, or on the garage forecourt, for example, the garage is responsible, unless it can prove that the damage was caused through no fault on its part. This is known as the law of bailment.

Service – delays

If you agree that work will be done by a specified time then the garage must keep to that time. If no time is agreed, under the Supply of Goods and Services Act 1982 the garage should carry out the work 'within a reasonable time'. So, if a garage takes six weeks to do what should take two (another garage may give an indication on what is reasonable), it is in breach of contract. Therefore, if an extra four weeks' car hire charges, say, were caused by the garage's delay, you should be able to recover those as damages for breach of contract – as long as the garage was aware that you would be hiring a car while yours was being repaired. The general rule is that you can recover only those items of loss which both parties could have contemplated at the time the contract was made as being likely to result from any breach. Unless you tell the trader that you will need to hire a car it might have assumed you would get the bus.

Service – unwanted work

Let's say you asked your local garage to give your car a 24,000 mile service, according to the manufacturer's guidelines. When you go to pay for the service, the garage tells you that it has also replaced the rear tyres because they were worn. This is not part of a 24,000-mile service, and you can probably get the tyres cheaper elsewhere. Is there anything you can do about this?

As you had a contract with the garage to service the car according to the manufacturer's guidelines for a 24,000-mile service, and no other work, you are entitled to tell the garage to remove the new tyres, put the old ones back on and reduce the bill accordingly. Practically, it might be easier to try and get the garage to reduce the bill for the tyres so that it matches the cheaper tyres mentioned, and you keep the tyres.

Service – price

No clear difference exists between an **estimate** and a **quotation** as the words do not have a legal definition. Nevertheless, there is an increasing tendency to give an estimate as a rough, provisional guide to the final price for the completed work, a quotation as a fixed price. So, if you find you are in dispute over a bill, the real issue is whether the price given was intended to be a rough-and-ready guide or fixed.

If a trader gives you a document with precise details of the work required with detailed costs, you should not be charged more once that work is done. The motor trade has a Code of Practice which follows this general tendency. So, if a dispute arises over the meaning of the words in an agreement, the relevant Code of Practice will provide a useful guideline. Before you finally agree a contract, make sure you get a written agreement and an **exact and firm quotation** for the work you are having done.

Agreeing a price with a garage for work is not always easy. The garage may not be quite sure what is wrong with a car until it starts work, and will not know how much the work is going to cost. But you do not have to accept whatever charge is made and you can limit the cost of the repair work.

When you ask a garage to do some work on your car, you only have to pay for the work that you have authorised. So, be clear about what you have agreed before allowing the garage to carry out any work, preferably by putting things in writing. If no fixed price is agreed, the law says that you are obliged to pay a 'reasonable price' for the work. This depends on how much work has been done and the type of repair or service undertaken. If you feel that the price you have been charged is too high, you will have to show that the price is unreasonable. So, get evidence from other garages or motoring organisations, if you are a member.

A useful tip is to ask the garage to give you an estimate once the problem has been diagnosed. Instead of just asking the garage to put your car right, ask it to tell you if the work is going to cost more than £300, say. If you are forced to pay as a condition of recovering your car, you should make it clear in writing that you are paying under protest and without prejudice to any legal rights you may have against the garage. This means that you can pursue the matter further when you have your car back.

If a garage has carried out repairs and improvements to your car, it has what in law is called a **repairer's lien** over the goods. It is legally entitled to hold on to the car until paid for the work. This can create problems, particularly as you may need to get another garage to look at the car in order to get evidence to challenge the bill, or the quality of the work. Check if the trader is a member of a trade association, and try and enlist that association's help in getting your car back. If that fails, you may have no option but to pay the bill **under protest** and recover your car – do this in writing, on the back of the cheque, say – and this will leave you free to claim back the disputed amount later. Again, contact the trade association, and consider the options of arbitration or taking the matter to court.

Delays

If you ask for work to be done to your car, the garage will tell you how long the work will take. If the work goes beyond the estimated time, and you have not made known any special circumstances which make the completion date vitally important, you cannot claim compensation. You can get around delays like this:

- if the work is not started or completed within a 'reasonable' time, you should write giving the company reasonable notice, imposing a deadline of one week, for example. If the work has not even been started, you can write imposing a similar deadline and treat the contract as at an end if the work is not done, recover your car, get the work done elsewhere, and claim back any extra costs incurred

- unless you have made time of the essence, in the absence of a notice imposing a strict time-limit in that way, you are legally obliged to continue with the contract and let the trader carry on with the work
- if you do wish a trader to do the job on or by a particular date and to be able to cancel otherwise, you must ensure that the agreed date is seen to be of importance by stressing that performance must occur precisely on time – make time 'of the essence'.

OTHER MATTERS

Dealing with franchises

Many car dealers are franchises, even though they have the logo and livery of a national company. Your contract is with the person or company who owned the franchise to that branch. If it is a franchise, it is legally obliged to display the name and address of the owner (usually by the door and on its letterhead). Although all the branches may be using the same logo and name, each one could be a different company. So, if the company that was running that particular branch has ceased trading, even though there are many other showrooms still trading with the same name, you cannot insist on the other branches dealing with your complaint. If a company goes bust, you are unlikely to recover compensation (see above), but if you paid on credit, you may have a claim against the credit company (see page 203).

Using credit

Credit can be a useful facility for buying expensive goods or just convenient for paying for goods and services. Some car dealers and manufacturers offer attractive-looking finance deals on their products. If you are not sure of all the costs of a credit deal, or you want more information than is in an advert, get a written quotation – legally you have to be given this if you ask for it. And when you fill in the application form make sure the details you give are correct; otherwise you may be breaking the law.

Most contracts become legally binding as soon as they are made, even if they are entirely verbal. However, a credit or hire agreement must *always* be in writing and the procedures are defined in the Consumer Credit Act 1974:

- the consumer signs a credit/hire purchase application form or the credit agreement itself (usually at the bank or finance company's premises, or in the car showroom) and retains a copy of the document signed. The creditor then checks the creditworthiness of the applicant – for example, by making enquiries with credit reference agencies. If all seems OK, the creditor will agree to grant the credit and will then sign the contract. The creditor must deliver to the applicant a **second copy** of the agreement form, signed by both parties, within seven days of the creditor signing
- if the customer signs at a bank or in the showroom, and the creditor signs at the *same* time, the agreement becomes legally binding there and then, and the customer is entitled to only **one copy** of the completed agreement
- where the form is signed by the consumer at home (or anywhere other than at the trader's or creditor's place of business), following face-to-face discussions between the customer and the trader, the situation is similar but the customer has a right to cancel the agreement during the 'cooling-off' period.

Generally you cannot get out of a contract simply because you have changed your mind. Whether you have a cooling-off period and so can cancel a credit agreement depends on *where* you made the agreement and whether it was signed by the trader at the same time you signed:

- if you signed at the showroom and the trader signed the credit agreement at the same time you cannot cancel (see above)

- some credit agreements do not come into force as soon as you sign, since the company also has to sign before the agreement becomes binding. The trader may want to run credit checks on you to see if you are a bad loan risk before going ahead. So if you change your mind you may be able to get out of the deal even if you signed the contract at the trader's premises. Tell the trader as soon as possible that you are withdrawing, before it has completed its credit checks and signed the agreement himself. Then you should have no problem
- if you signed face-to-face with the trader at your home or at a friend's, you have a right to cancel. But you must act quickly. The 'cooling-off' period lasts for five clear days. When you sign up for the credit you must be given a **notice of your cancellation rights** along with a copy of the credit agreement, and you have five days to send your cancellation in writing. The five days does not start to run until you receive the **second copy** of the agreement from the company with a notice of your cancellation rights. Both copies of the agreement must mention the right of cancellation. The **second copy** must be delivered **by post**. The countdown to the fifth day of the cooling-off period does not begin until the debtor has **received** the **second copy** and does not include that day. If the trader does not comply with the formal procedures set down by the Consumer Credit Act 1974, the whole deal cannot be enforced by the company.

To cancel, you must give written notice to the creditor or an agent who conducted the negotiations, such as the salesman. If you mail the cancellation, it will take effect as soon as it is posted, so make sure you get a certificate of posting from the Post Office. The effect of cancellation is to bring the whole agreement to an end and to absolve you from any future liability. If you have paid a deposit, that must be refunded to you.

Credit – early repayment

With most credit agreements you can repay early. If you want to repay a fixed-term loan early, the lender can charge you a certain proportion of the extra interest and charges you would have paid if you had stuck with the loan for the full term. Generally, the longer the loan and the earlier you settle, the higher the charge. The most common way to exercise your right of early settlement is to send written notice to the creditor. The creditor is obliged to send a statement, free of charge, setting out the amount required to pay off the loan after taking account of the rebate allowable. The statement must set out the basic calculations involved in arriving at that sum. You can then pay off all you owe under the agreement, less the rebate.

Credit – extra protection

Buying on credit can also offer some additional protection – it depends on what form of credit you use. In short, there has to be some 'connection' between the trader and the finance company – for example, if you entered into a credit agreement that was arranged by the garage that sold you the car, then under s75 of the Consumer Credit Act 1974 the credit company is also liable for any breach of contract or misrepresentation for which the garage would be liable. This is called 'joint and several liability'. So, if the car was unmerchantable and you could have demanded a refund or the cost of repair from the retailer, you can claim exactly the same from the finance company.

This protection comes into its own where the trader you are complaining against goes **out of business**. There may be a practical problem if the seller goes bust before your car arrives, say, or before your dispute is settled. It is a sad fact that when a company goes bust consumers often lose out. Let us say your car has broken down after only a couple of months. If you paid in cash, it is unlikely you will get any compensation for your losses (the cost of repair, say). When a business collapses and cannot pay all its debts, there is a strict order of who gets paid first. As an ordinary customer, you are what is known as an unsecured creditor and unfortunately you come at the back of the queue behind other 'preferential creditors' like company employees who are owed salary, the Inland Revenue or those who have secured loans to the company. You will miss any chance of getting your money back if you do not get in the queue quickly, so contact the receiver or liquidator straight away. Often there is not enough money to go around so you could end up getting nothing at all.

If you are paying any money up front but not driving the car away with you, make sure you know where your goods are, and insist that they are marked with your name. If they are clearly labelled as yours, go to the showroom or warehouse and try to collect them. But if they have not been marked as yours, they are just one indistinguishable part of a large batch, so you cannot prove that any particular one is the one you ordered.

Arranging a loan through your local bank to pay for a car may get you a good flexible deal, but you will not be able to pursue the bank under s75 of the Consumer Credit Act. The bank is an 'unconnected' lender and has nothing effectively to do with the purchase of the car. In this case you have two hopes: one is that as one of the creditors of the garage, there will be some money left over to pay your claim – this is unlikely; the other is that any manufacturer's guarantee will cover your claim – you will have to look at the wording of the guarantee to see whether or not your claim is covered.

Hire purchase and conditional sale finance

If the finance is in the form of a hire purchase or conditional sale agreement your contract of sale is with the finance company and not the retailer. When you buy in this way your legal rights are against the finance company which lends you the money, *not* the retailer with which you originally dealt. This is because in effect the retailer sells the car to the finance company and it then sells or hires the car on to you. The goods do not legally become yours as soon as you start paying, and usually do not become yours until you have paid all the instalments. So, if you have been sold faulty goods, your rights are as follows:

- you have the same basic rights as if you had paid cash. With HP these rights are laid down by the Supply of Goods (Implied Terms) Act 1973. As is the case with ordinary purchases this Act says that goods supplied on HP must be of **merchantable quality**, **fit for their purpose**, and correspond with any **description** given of them

- when it comes to rejecting faulty goods your rights to ask for your money back last longer if you bought on HP than if you have bought them for cash – on HP you have the common law right to reject faulty goods *throughout* the duration of the agreement
- you should contact the finance company saying the car is unmerchantable, that you are réjecting it, and that it is available for collection by the company
- you are then entitled to get back any instalments you have paid and you do not have to pay any more
- you are not compelled to reject the car. If you want to keep it, but would like a free repair, say, write to the finance company saying what is wrong, what you want it to do about it, and that you will continue paying only 'under protest' until things are put right
- you are entitled to claim compensation for any expenses you incur which were reasonably foreseeable by both you and the company at the time you entered the HP agreement – for example, the cost of alternative means of transport while your car was being repaired
- once you have paid all the instalments on your goods, your rights become the same as if you had paid cash.

If you currently have your car on hire purchase, you cannot sell it until you have paid off all the instalments. The car is still owned by the finance company, and you will own it only when you have paid off all the instalments and purchased it. You only have the right to *use* the car until then. If you do sell, you will automatically be in breach of your obligations as a seller under the Sale of Goods Act 1979. That Act says that you must own the car (i.e. have title to the car) before you sell. You would also be liable to the finance company for wrongfully selling property that belongs to it. The situation is entirely different where you have bought goods on credit using a loan or credit card, as you will become the owner of the goods as soon as you start paying.

Miscellaneous problems

Imagine you are driving along a road in winter when your car is showered with grit from the council gritting lorry or damaged by a pothole in the road. Or you park your car in the street next to some scaffolding where decorating work is being done and return to find paint splattered over the roof and bonnet. You will want to claim compensation from the person responsible. The council or the decorating company may refuse to accept liability for their employees.

If an employee, acting in the course of his or her employment, causes you to suffer damage or loss, you are entitled to claim compensation from that person's employer. As long as you can prove that the damage was in fact caused by the employee, you should write to the council or company and send details of the damage caused. If they will not pay up you will have to consider either making a claim on your own car insurance, or taking the claim to court.

If you are injured or your property is damaged as a result of the carelessness of others, you can claim compensation:

- the council or company employees owe you and other passers-by a duty of care not to cause any damage when carrying out their work – for example, they should take precautions to shield pedestrians and road-users from paint and debris, and not throw grit around in a careless way
- your claim will be against the council, company or business which employed the workmen, rather than the individual workmen, so you should make sure you address your written complaint to the managing director or partners as appropriate
- they could argue that you **contributed** to the damage, by parking too close to the work, driving too fast or without paying attention, say. There may have been parking restrictions or other warning notices in the area which you did not spot. If this is the case, then any compensation you get will be reduced to reflect your own lack of care – a court would be able to divide up responsibility accordingly. If the repairs to your car cost £600, say, the court may decide that you were 50 per cent to blame, and you would only recover £300.

COMPLAINING

The following points should help you to make an effective complaint in most circumstances. We also list the most common excuses you may come up against when you do complain, and tell you how to deal with them.

- **Act quickly** Do not let your complaint go stale. If you discover a defect in a car or a problem with a service go straight back to the trader, or if that is inconvenient, write.
- **Know your rights** Check in this book what you are entitled to so you can let the person to whom you are complaining know the legal basis of your claim.
- **Target your complaint** Write or insist on speaking to someone in authority – the manager if it is a local branch or the managing director if it is a company. Do not vent your anger on the telephonist or the salesroom staff – the chances are they will not have the authority to make a decision about the problem.
- **Keep a record of your action** Even if you complain in person, or by telephone, make sure you keep a record of what was said and when, together with a note of the name and position of the person you dealt with.
- **Follow up in writing** Unless your problem is resolved immediately, follow up your complaint by letter. Sending your letter to a named individual reduces the risk of it being passed around the organisation and perhaps being ignored or lost. Type the letter (or write as neatly as possible), date it, and, if appropriate, give the letter a heading (the invoice number, say). Use this heading, and any reference given by the organisation, every time you write.

  To avoid committing yourself by mistake when negotiating settlement terms, write '**without prejudice**' at the top of your letter, but do not use it on all your letters – this may cause problems later as you may not be able to use these in court.

  You may be sent a cheque in **full and final settlement** of your claim. Be very careful here – even if you do not accept the money but cash the cheque, there is a danger you will be prevented from claiming more.

- **Keep to the point** A brief letter setting out the facts in short paragraphs, rather than an angry or emotional letter making personal remarks, will help your claim. But be firm. By quoting the relevant law – the Sale of Goods Act 1979 if you are complaining about faulty goods or the Supply of Goods and Services Act 1982 in respect of inadequate services, for example – you show you are aware of your rights and mean business. State what redress you want – if you want your money back, a repair or a replacement, or if you want financial compensation, spell it out. Give a reasonable deadline for a response – 14 days for a simple matter, but longer if it's a more substantial problem such as major repair work. Use recorded delivery and keep copies of all your correspondence and documents.
- **Get evidence** Get and keep any evidence you can to support your claim: for example, receipts, invoices, brochures, contract terms and conditions, advertisements, estimates, bills, statements from witnesses, evidence from other traders as to 'reasonable' charges, photographs of damage, and technical expert evidence if appropriate.
- **Be persistent and do not be fobbed-off** If you are not happy with the response to your complaint, or you have got no response at all, write another letter. Do not fall prey to attempts to fob you off with less than you are entitled to. Here are some of the most common ones:
  - **'You're too late, you must complain within 30 days'** Do not accept time limits like this. Whether it is goods or services you are complaining about, your rights to claim compensation for breach of contract or negligence last for six years (five years in Scotland), and three years in personal injury claims. So, even if you have lost the right to reject faulty goods, say, because the 'reasonable' period of time has elapsed, you can still claim compensation. Even if there is a term in a contract, such as extended warranty, and you do not complain within the set time limit, you may be able to challenge this under the Unfair Contract Terms Act 1977.
  - **'We don't give refunds'** If you have bought spare parts or accessories for your car, say, that are faulty, unfit for their

purpose or not as described, you are entitled to a refund if you act quickly enough. Notices saying 'No refunds given' are against the law, so do not be put off by them, and report any to the local trading standards department (see Addresses).

- **'We don't guarantee our products'** You can ignore this. Your rights as a consumer in all circumstances apply whether you have a written guarantee or not (see page 180).
- **'*You* caused the problem, not us'** Do not be deterred by this. For example, the seat fabric in your car should be designed to withstand the normal use, so if it rips or wears out soon after purchase the trader cannot blame the way you used the seats. But if it is not as clear-cut as this, you may need an independent test on the product or service.
- **'It's not our problem, try the manufacturer'** If you have bought something faulty, it is up to the retailer to deal with it, not the manufacturer. But all too often the retailer will try to pass you on to the manufacturer or force you to claim on the manufacturer's guarantee on the grounds that 'we only sell them'. Do not accept this and tell the retailer that the legal responsibility rests with them. This also applies to complaints about items supplied by somebody doing work for you – for example, a repairer or servicing garage.
- **'We can't do anything without a receipt'** There is no legal requirement to have a receipt, but you may have to prove when and where you paid for the goods or service. So, if the trader asks for proof of payment, a receipt is useful. But a credit card voucher, say, would be legally acceptable.
- **'No refunds on sale items'** If you buy goods like car accessories in a sale you still have your normal rights. If you buy seconds, you cannot expect them to be perfect, but they must still be of merchantable quality (i.e. free from hidden defects) and as described. But you cannot complain about any defects which were pointed out to you or which you should have spotted before buying.

• **Be reasonable** Be prepared to come to a compromise if you receive a fair offer, even if it is not exactly what you wanted. But be warned that once you've accepted an offer of compensation you cannot ask for more later.

Following the right complaints procedure

Failure to agree with the trader means it is time to let somebody else decide on the rights and wrongs of your complaint. Many car dealers, servicing garages and manufacturers are members of trade associations which operate the various motor industry codes of practice. These associations have free conciliation services which will try to settle the dispute.

If the company or trader you are dealing with does not answer your letters, or refuses to sort your problem out, do not be discouraged from pursuing your complaint further. If a member company has breached the terms of the code, inform the trade association as it may be able to persuade the trader to comply. There is no guarantee that it will follow a particular code; the trade association can only put pressure on members to comply, it cannot force them to do so. But if members do not follow the code, they risk being thrown out of the association and losing the benefits that brings them. The associations offer free **conciliation** in disagreements between consumers and member companies, and **arbitration** schemes to sort out disputes.

In some situations one of the many **ombudsman** schemes will provide a means of settling your dispute as an alternative to going to court. Those most likely to cover disputes arising from ownership of your car are the Banking Ombudsman, the Building Societies Ombudsman and the Insurance Ombudsman (see Addresses). The schemes are completely free and aim to be less complex and time-consuming than legal proceedings, in many cases upholding the spirit and not just the letter of the law.

Court is nearly always available, but should be considered only as a last resort. Court action can be lengthy and costly, and legal aid is available only to a few. The **small claims procedure** provides an admirable and low-cost way of using the courts with its informal and simplified procedures. As long as you have a genuine dispute with a company or trader, you can claim through the courts. However, even if the amount of your claim is below the small claims limit of £1,000 (£750 in Scotland) you should try to sort the matter out by using the alternative methods first – so contact any relevant trade association and ask if it will conciliate, or, if it is a problem over a finance or insurance claim, refer the matter to the appropriate ombudsman. If that proves unsuccessful, you will then have to decide between arbitration and court. If you do choose to start legal proceedings, you need to send one last letter to the company, stating that if it does not sort the dispute out within a reasonable time, usually 7 to 14 days, you will issue a county court summons. Such a letter is known as a '**letter before action**'. If you have not heard from the company within the time limit, you can issue proceedings.

How do these procedures work?

Trade associations

The logo of the trade association should be displayed prominently at the trader's place of business and is usually displayed on its headed notepaper. The main associations for the motor industry are the Society of Motor Manufacturers and Traders (SMMT), which represents the vast majority of vehicle manufacturers, the Retail Motor Industry Federation (RMI) and the Scottish Motor Trade Association (SMTA), which cover car dealers, accessories retailers and servicing garages:

- you should check with the association that the membership is genuine
- if there is no indication anywhere that the trader is a member of an association, contact the trade association which seems most likely to apply (see Addresses)
- ask the trader if it is a member of a trade association, or
- contact the Office of Fair Trading (see Addresses).

Conciliation

This is usually offered by the trade association to which the trader belongs and the association will try to bring you and the trader together to reach a mutually acceptable compromise. Conciliation is free and informal and may result in the settlement of the dispute. It is often a prerequisite to arbitration in that many trade associations insist on the use of conciliation facilities before the dispute can be referred to their arbitration scheme. However, the outcome of conciliation is not legally binding and the trade association cannot force its members to reach a compromise. If conciliation does not resolve the dispute, you can still go to court or refer the dispute to arbitration.

Arbitration

Any dispute can be sorted out by arbitration, whether through a scheme operated under a trade association code of practice (**code arbitration**), or by arranging it yourself independently of any association. Arbitration schemes are operated by independent bodies like the Chartered Institute of Arbitrators (see Addresses). The arbitrators appointed are independent of the trade association and are usually qualified professionals, such as surveyors, architects, engineers and lawyers.

In all cases, you can refer the matter to arbitration only if both sides agree. You and the trader will each put your side of the story to an independent person, an arbitrator (arbiter in Scotland), whose decision will be binding on both of you. Although the procedure is informal, a fee of some kind is payable. Most of the costs arising from arbitration schemes operated for trade associations are borne by the trader or trade association, and consequently your costs tend to be relatively low. It is best to deal with traders who are members of trade associations so you keep all your options open.

The special arbitration schemes run by the motor industry trade associations are a cheap alternative to court, and may be worth considering if you do not want to take your dispute to court. If conciliation fails, therefore, you can choose arbitration – what you will have to pay depends on the amount you are claiming (generally between a minimum of £35 + VAT and a maximum of £69 plus VAT, although you should get this back if you win).

If you arrange your own arbitration hearing independently your costs could be quite high. You can contact the Chartered Institute of Arbitrators (see Addresses) and ask it to arbitrate if a cheap special code scheme is not available. But the arbitrator will charge out his or her time at an hourly rate and the loser will pay – this rate depends on the type and complexity of the problem.

Using arbitration instead of court is always an option:

- you cannot be forced to go to arbitration. The Consumer Arbitration Agreements Act 1988 outlaws contract terms which state that disputes below £1,000 must be referred to arbitration – these are not legally binding
- arbitration schemes are offered as alternatives to court, not in addition to it, so you have to choose
- arbitration schemes generally use written evidence only, so you cannot present your case in person – it is not always easy to put your problem clearly in writing. Court gives you the opportunity to put your side of the case
- once you have made your choice, the decision of the judge or arbitrator is binding, so you cannot have the case reheard using the other option if you are unhappy with the decision.

Small claims court

Claims of £1,000 or less (in England, Wales and Northern Ireland) or £750 or less in Scotland, are known as small claims. Such claims are automatically referred by the court to 'small claims arbitration' in what is commonly known as the **small claims court** and are heard by a district judge. Although this is rather confusingly called 'arbitration' it is completely different from arbitration schemes run by trade associations and organised by bodies like the Chartered Institute of Arbitrators. The small claims court is part of the county court (Sheriff Court in Scotland) but it uses simplified rules, which makes it fairly straightforward for people using it.

Which court and what does it cost?

You can start the claim (**issue** proceedings) in your local county court. But if the person or company you are suing defends the case, then it will automatically be transferred to a county court nearer the defendant's home or place of business. Many cases settle out of court, but the main advantage of the small claims court is cost. You won't have to seek the assistance of a solicitor, so you will not incur solicitors' charges as the informal process is designed for you to represent yourself.

If you win, you will get back:

- the court fee
- your own and your witnesses, reasonable expenses incurred travelling to and from the hearing
- your own and your witnesses' loss of earnings of £29 each
- up to £112.50 if you paid an expert (an engineer, say) to provide evidence to support your case.

Even if you lose, the only costs which can normally be awarded against you are:

- the defendants' and their witnesses' reasonable expenses incurred travelling to and from the hearing
- up to £29 each to cover the money the defendants and their witnesses would have earned that day
- up to £112.50 to cover the cost of any expert fees.

Claims over £1,000 are dealt with in the full county court (over £750 in the Sheriff Court in Scotland). These are subject to formal rules of evidence, and unless you have had experience of presenting cases in court and cross-examination you would be at a severe disadvantage. Legal representation, although not compulsory, is therefore usually essential, and as a result you will have to ask a solicitor to act for you. Furthermore, unlike in small claims cases, if you lose your case you face the prospect of having to pay not only your own solicitor's costs but also the other side's lawyer's bill, which could run into several thousands of pounds. Therefore, proceedings in the full county court can turn out to be very expensive.

Even if the amount involved is over the small claims limit you can still have the case handled as a small claims arbitration. Either side must apply to the court and the court must agree. This way you can still benefit from the informal procedures. However, if you lose, you will have to pay the other side's costs, as in the full county court. Alternatively, you can limit your claim to £1,000 and make full use of the benefits of the small claims court. But you will have to accept that you will not recover any extra.

Free leaflets explaining what to do are available from county courts. You can also obtain a **default summons** from your local county court. There are two forms: Form N1, which you should use when claiming a fixed amount, or Form N2, which you should use when you are not claiming a specific amount.

The court forms have recently been simplified so you should not have too much trouble filling them in. If you do need any assistance, the court staff, your local Citizens Advice Bureau or Consumer Advice Centre will help you. Some points to remember:

- it is important that you sue the right person or company – a name on a letterhead, for example, may only be the trading name, not the real registered company name
- check that the trader is still in business by contacting the Trading Standards Department for the area local to the business, or, if it is a company, telephone Companies House (see Addresses)
- you will have to pay an issue fee ranging from a minimum of £10 to £65 for claims over £1,000.

Arbitration versus court

The advantages of having your claim dealt with by arbitration are as follows:

- generally there is no hearing to attend so you will not have to take time off work or incur travel expenses
- if you are worried about presenting your case in person, choose arbitration as it is based on documents only
- financial limits are usually more than the small claims court limit of £1,000.

The disadvantages are:

- you will not be able to argue your case in person
- it is not always easy to put the extent of your problem in writing and include all relevant facts
- the trader must be a member of the relevant trade association to enable you to use a code scheme, otherwise arbitration could be expensive.

The advantages of pursuing a claim through the small claims court are:

- costs
- you present your own case in an informal hearing. It may be easier for you to get across the extent of your case by giving a verbal account of your troubles
- it is relatively easy to make a claim
- issuing a summons shows you mean business and often leads to a sensible offer.

The disadvantages of court action are:

- you will need to take time off work to attend the hearing
- you will incur travel expenses
- you will have to present your own case at the hearing, which some people may find difficult and daunting
- there is a financial limit in the small claims court of £1,000 (£750 in Scotland).

Enforcement

Even if you win your case and get a judgment there is no guarantee that you will get your money. If you do not, you will probably have to take further court action. The various procedures open to you are set out and explained in a free booklet from your local county court. The court will do nothing at all on its own initiative so it is up to you to take enforcement action and to choose the best method. The key to successful enforcement is to find out what assets there are and to select a method of enforcement to get at them. The methods of enforcement are as follows:

- **Attachment of earnings** This enforces payment from the wages salary of an employed (as opposed to a self-employed) judgment debtor. The employers are obliged to make specified deductions from pay on a week-by-week or month-by-month basis and pay it to the court.
- **Warrant of execution** This orders bailiffs to remove and sell sufficient goods belonging to the judgment debtor to pay the debt. Items on hire purchase or belonging to someone else

cannot be seized. The judgment debtor's clothes, bedding and trade tools up to a certain value cannot be seized.

- **Garnishee proceedings** This directs moneys that are due to the judgment debtor to be paid to you instead. For example, it can be used in relation to money held in the judgment debtor's bank or building society account or a trade debt.
- **Charging order** This can be placed on property, whether the home or business premises, owned by the judgment debtor, by himself or jointly with someone else. The object of such an order is to have the property sold to pay the judgment debt.

If you do not know anything about the financial position of the judgment debtor or his business it may be in your best interests to find out as much as you can on this before opting for one of the above methods of enforcement. You can do this by applying to the court for an **oral examination of the judgment debtor's means**. This procedure allows you, or the court, to ask the debtor a series of questions to find out how much money/assets he has and how much he can afford to pay. Once you have got such information it will then be easier for you to decide whether it is worth enforcing the judgment and if so, the best method.

Further help and advice

If you cannot resolve your dispute with the help of this book, there are many other sources of help and advice:

- read *120 Letters that Get Results* or *350 Legal Problems Solved* (Which? Books)
- contact your local Citizens Advice Bureau (CAB) or Consumer Advice Centre or Law Centre – their advice is free
- contact a solicitor who can give you advice under a pre-arranged fixed-fee interview – you should be able to get about half an hour's advice for a small fee. Ring the solicitors in your area to check if this scheme is part of the services they offer.

ADDRESSES

Accident Legal Service (ALAS)
The Law Society, Freepost, London WC2A 1BR
071-242 2430

Association of British Insurers (ABI)
51–55 Gresham Street, London EC2V 7HQ
071-928 7600

Association of Personal Injury Lawyers (APIL)
10a Byard Lane, Nottingham NG1 2GJ
(0602) 580585

Automobile Association (AA)
Fanum House, Basing View, Basingstoke, Hants RG21 2EA
(0256) 20123

The Banking Ombudsman
70 Gray's Inn Road, London WC1X 8BN
071-404 9944

British Insurance and Investment Brokers Association (BIIBA)
BIIBA House, 14 Bevis Marks, London EC3A 7NT
071-623 9043

The Building Societies Ombudsman
Grosvenor Gardens House, 35–37 Grosvenor Gardens, London SW1X 7AW
071-931 0044

Chartered Institute of Arbitrators
24 Angel Gate, City Road, London EC1V 2RS
071-837 4483

Companies House
Crown Way, Cardiff CF4 3UZ
(0222) 380801

Consumers' Association
2 Marylebone Road, London NW1 4DF
071-830 6000

DVLC
Swansea SA99 1BR
(0792) 772151

HP Information plc
Dolphin House, PO Box 61, New Street, Salisbury, Wiltshire SP1 2TB
(0722) 422422

Institute of Advanced Motorists (IAM)
IAM House, 359 Chiswick High Road, London W4 4HS
081-994 4403

Institute of Automotive Engineer Assessors
18 St Thomas Road, Brentwood, Essex CM14 4DB
(0277) 222709

Insurance Ombudsman Bureau
135 Park Street, London SE1 9EA
071-928 7600

Motor Insurers Bureau (MIB)
New Garden House, 78 Hatton Gardens, London EC1N 8JQ
071-242 0033

Office of Fair Trading
Field House, Bream's Buildings, London EC4A 1PR
071-242 2858

Personal Insurance Arbitration Service (PIAS)
(see Chartered Institute of Arbitrators)

Retail Motor Industry Federation
The National Conciliation Service, 9 North Street,
Rugby CV21 2AB
(0788) 576465

Retail Motor Industry Federation (head office)
201 Great Portland Street, London W1N 6AB
071-580 9122

Royal Automobile Club (RAC)
RAC House, PO Box 100, Bartlett Street, S. Croydon,
Surrey CR2 6XW
081-686 0088

Royal Society for the Prevention of Accidents (RoSPA)
The Priory Queensway, Cannon House, Birmingham B4 6BS
021-200 2461

Scottish Motor Trade Association
3 Palmerston Place, Edinburgh EH12 5AF
031-225 3643

Society of Motor Manufacturers and Traders
Forbes House, Halkin Street, London SW1X 7DX
071-235 7000

Trading Standards Departments
Contact the department at the offices of the council local to the trader you are complaining about – in the phone book under 'council'.

Vehicle Builders and Repairers Association
Belmont House, 102 Finkle Lane, Gildersome, Leeds LS27 7TW
(0532) 538333

APPENDIX 1

WHICH? BEST BUYS

Which? Best Buys are divided into the four major categories of car. They are good all-rounders and good value for money. None is perfect but they are likely to satisfy most buyers looking for a car of this type. This list comprises current models, which can be bought new or used, as well as some cars which are discontinued but still available second-hand.

A *Which?* Best Buy car must:

- score an above-average, or at the very least average, reliability rating. Where a car is too new for reliability information, the record of the make as a whole is looked at
- score a secondary safety rating at least average for that class of car
- rate well for ease of driving, ease of using controls, comfort, performance and space
- be good value for money, taking into account equipment and features provided as standard.

The following are the Best Buys from the *Which? Guide to New and Used Cars 1994*.

SUPERMINIS

1994 *Which?* Best Buy

Nissan Micra

1994 *Which?* Runners-up

Daihatsu Charade
Peugeot 106
Rover Metro (May 1990 onwards)
Toyota Starlet
Vauxhall Corsa
Vauxhall Nova (used only)

1994 Best-selling model

Ford Fiesta

SMALL FAMILY CARS

1994 *Which?* Best Buys

Rover 200/400
Mazda 323

1994 *Which?* Runners-up

Honda Concerto
Nissan Sunny
Proton MPi
Toyota Corolla
VW Golf/Vento

1994 Best-selling model

Ford Escort

LARGE FAMILY CARS

1994 *Which?* Best Buys

Nissan Primera
Toyota Carina E

1994 *Which?* Runners-up

Audi 80
BMW 3 Series (new shape)
Citroën Xantia
Honda Accord
Mazda 626 (pre-March 1992, used only)

Mitsubishi Galant
Rover 600
Toyota Carina

1994 Best-selling model
Ford Mondeo

EXECUTIVE CARS

1994 *Which?* Best Buy
No overall choice

1994 *Which?* Recommended
Audi 100 (May 1991 onwards)
BMW 5 Series (March 1988 onwards)
Mercedes 190
Saab 900s 2.0i
Toyota Camry
Volvo 850

1994 Best-selling model
Rover 800

APPENDIX 2

Approved Security Devices

The insurance industry tests car security devices for approval to its own set of standards of reliability and security. The list below is the fourth produced, in July 1994. You can get a copy of this and updates by sending a large stamped addressed envelope to Department VS, 51 Gresham Street, London EC2V 7HQ.

Category 1

Type of device: Combined alarm/immobiliser

Key features:

- Alarm with full perimetric and volumetric detection, stand-by power supply
- Immobiliser isolating a minimum of two circuits, passively armed
- Anti-scan, anti-grab resistance of codes

Approved devices:

Make/model	Approx. cost fitted
CEL Topline 3011	£434
CEL Topline 3016	£449
Cobra 6019	£475
Laserline 996	£385
Nissan NATS V1.0 Plus	standard fit
Gemini 5160T	£450
Selmar SBA 598	£450

Spyball SPK 660	£450
Foxguard H2-M	£250
Foxguard F1-11	£400
Scorpion 2000	varies
Toyota 5000	£475

Category 2

Type of device: Electronic/electromechanical immobiliser

Key features:
- Immobiliser isolating a minimum of two circuits, passively armed
- Anti-scan, anti-grab resistance of codes

Approved devices:	Make/model	Approx. cost fitted
General	AA Immobiliser	£140
	BMW MB Immobiliser	£200
	Cartec Guardsman 2000	£160
	CEL Protector 10	£140
	CEL Protector 15	£155
	CEL Protector 20	£165
	Gemel Serpi Star MK125	£180
	Gemini Falco 5049	£200
	Gemini GAT	£300
	Hamilton & Palmer Matrix 2	£150
	Hamilton & Palmer Matrix 3	£210
	Hamilton & Palmer Vantage ATS	£300
	Laserline 992T	£120
	Technology for Today – Meridian 250	£230
For specific cars	Ferrari Immobiliser	£350
	Ford 951	£225
	Jaguar ERC	£500
	Mazda MVSS 115	£160
	Porsche Immobiliser	£400
	Vauxhall VIM 129	POA

Fitted as standard	Ford Security System – Escort Cosworth Ford Safeguard – Fiesta, Escort Nissan NATS V1.0 – some Nissans

Category 3

Type of device: Mechanical Immobiliser

Key features:

- Immobiliser isolating a minimum of one operating system
- Easy to arm and disarm
- Attack resistance to five minutes minimum using comprehensive range of hand tools
- Can be permanently fitted, or used as a temporary supplementary device, or as security on lower-risk vehicles

Approved devices:

Make/model	Approx. cost fitted
Barrier Deadlock	£150
Carflow Longarm	£50
Vauxhall Steering Wheel Bar	£50
AA High Security Steering Lock	£50
ABUS Carblock Granit	£50
Mul-T-Lock 22	£175
Vauxhall Gearlock	£175

APPENDIX 3

SECONDARY SAFETY SCORES

The cars are split into four classes and listed with the safest car in the class first. While, generally, the heavier the car you are in, the better off you will be in a crash, the scores can be compared across classes – a Vauxhall Corsa Supermini (score 6) gives a similar level of protection in an accident to an executive Citroën XM. Within each rating models are ranked in order of safety scores.

SUPERMINIS

6	Vauxhall Corsa 1.2i Merit	Sep 93
6	Vauxhall Nova 1.3 L	Sep 88
5	Seat Ibiza 1.3 CLXi	Jun 94
5	VW Polo 1.3 C Formel E	Aug 86
5	Ford Fiesta 1.1 CFi	Sep 93
5	Ford Fiesta XR2i	Feb 91
5	Nissan Micra 1.0L	Sep 93
5	Rover Metro 1.4 L auto	Jan 93
5	Ford Fiesta 1.3i LX auto	Jan 93
5	Rover Metro GTi 16v	Feb 91
5	Toyota Starlet 1.0GL	Aug 86
5	Daihatsu Charade 1.3 GXi	Jun 94
5	Ford Fiesta 1.1 L	Sep 89
5	Toyota Starlet 1.3 GLi	Sep 93
5	Toyota Starlet 1.0 GL	Jun 92
4	Rover Metro 1.1 S	Jan 91
4	Renault Clio 1.4 RT auto	Jan 93
4	Fiat Uno 60S	Jan 91
4	Suzuki Swift 1.3 GTi	Feb 91
4	Fiat Uno Turbo i.e.	Feb 91
4	Renault Clio 1.2 RL Prima	Feb 93
4	Vauxhall Nova 1.0 Saloon	Aug 86
4	Peugeot 106 XT 1.1	Jun 92
4	Subaru Vivio GLi 4WD	Feb 94
4	Renault Clio 1.4 RN	Jun 91
4	Renault 5 1.2 TR	Sep 88
4	Peugeot 205 1.6 GTi	Feb 91
4	Fiat Uno 60 DS	Feb 89
4	Ford Fiesta 1.1 L auto	Apr 88
4	Suzuki Swift 1.3 GLX	Jun 90
4	Nissan Micra 1.2 GSX	Jun 90

4	Daihatsu Mira	Feb 94
4	VW Polo Coupé 1.3 CL	Jun 92
4	Daihatsu Charade 1.0 CX	Sep 88
4	Fiat Uno Selecta	Apr 88
4	Fiat Panda 1000 S	Mar 89
4	Fiat Uno 45	Aug 86
4	Renault 5 1.4 auto	Apr 88
4	Renault 5 1.1 TL	Aug 86
4	Suzuki Swift 1.3 GS	Aug 86
4	Fiat Cinquecento (LHD)	Feb 94
4	Peugeot 205 1.6 Auto	Apr 88
4	Fiat Panda 750 L	Aug 87
4	Metro 1.0 City	Mar 89
4	Mini City	Feb 87
4	Peugeot 205 1.4 GR	Aug 86
3	Citroën AX 14 TRS	Sep 88
3	Citroën AX 1.1i Echo	Sep 93
3	Citroën AX 11 RE	Aug 87

SMALL FAMILY CARS

8	Vauxhall Astra 1.6i GLS	Jun 93
7	Vauxhall Astra 1.4i LS	May 92
7	Rover 218 SD	Jan 92
6	Rover 416 GSi	Jun 91
6	Rover 216 SLi auto	Jan 93
6	Rover 214 Si 16v	Jul 90
6	Toyota Corolla 1.6 GL est	Apr 90
6	VW Vento 2.0 GL	Jun 93
6	Ford Orion 1.6 EFi Ghia	Mar 91
6	Volvo 340 1.7 GL	Apr 87
6	VW Golf 1.8 GL	Sep 92
6	Ford Orion LX 1.8i 16v	Oct 92
6	VW Golf 1.4 CL	Sep 92
6	Ford Escort 1.8 LD	Jan 92
6	Subaru Impreza 1.8 GL	Jun 94
5	Honda Concerto 1.6i	Oct 92
5	Fiat Tipo 1.7D	Jan 92
5	Peugeot 306 1.6 XR	Jun 94
5	Nissan Sunny 1.6 LX auto	Jan 93
5	Toyota Corolla 1.3 GLi	Jun 93
5	Renault 19 GTD	Jan 92
5	Vauxhall Belmont 1.3 L	Apr 87
5	Toyota Corolla 1.3 GL	Jan 89
5	Mitsubshi Colt 1.6 GLXi	Jun 93
5	Alfa Romeo 33 1.7 i.e.	Jun 91
5	Ford Escort 1.4 LX	Mar 91
5	Nissan Sunny 1.6 SLX	Oct 92
5	Citroën ZX Aura 1.6i auto	Jan 93
5	Renault 19 TXE Chamade	Oct 92
5	Seat Toledo 1.8 GLXi	Oct 92
5	Renault 19 1.4 GTS	Sep 89
5	Nissan Sunny 1.4 LS	May 92
5	Hyundai Lantra 1.6 GLS	Oct 92
5	VW Golf 1.3 C	Apr 87
5	Honda Civic 1.5 LSi	Oct 92
5	Citroën ZX 1.4 Reflex	May 92
5	Mazda 323 1.6 SE Exec	Jun 91
5	Fiat Tipo 1.4 DGT	Sep 89
5	Ford Escort 1.4 L	Apr 87
5	Nissan Sunny 1.6 GS	Jun 90
5	Proton 1.5 GLS	Jun 90
5	Honda Civic 1.3 DX auto	Apr 88
5	Mazda 323 1.3 LX	Feb 88
5	Daihatsu Applause 1.6 Xi	Jun 91
5	Mazda 323 1.3 LX	Apr 87
5	Honda Civic 1.3 DX 16v	Jan 89
5	Rover Maestro 1.6	Oct 87
4	Peugeot 309 1.3 GL	Apr 87
4	Nissan Sunny 1.3 LX	Feb 88
4	Honda Ballade EX	Feb 88
4	Lada Samara 1300 SL	Mar 89
4	Peugeot 309 GRD	Jan 92

4	Rover 216 S	Oct 87
4	Skoda Favorit 136 LX	Jun 90
4	Rover 213 S	Jan 86

LARGE FAMILY CARS

10	Ford Mondeo 1.8i GLX	Mar 94
8	Audi 80 2.0	Mar 93
8	Vauxhall Cavalier 2.0i 4x4	Apr 90
7	BMW 316i auto	Jan 93
7	BMW 316i	Jun 92
7	Vauxhall Cavalier 1.8i GLa	Jan 93
7	Vauxhall Cavalier 2.0 GLi	Aug 89
7	VW Passat CL dsl Estate	Nov 89
7	Audi 80 1.8E	Nov 87
7	Vauxhall Cavalier 1.6 L	Aug 89
7	VW Passat 1.8 CL	Nov 88
6	Volvo 440 GLi	Jan 90
6	Volvo 460 GLi	Oct 91
6	Toyota Carina E 2.0 GLi	Mar 93
6	Nissan Primera 2.0 SLX	Mar 93
6	Citroën Xantia 1.8i SX	Mar 94
6	Audi 80 1.8 GL	Oct 86
6	Honda Accord 2.0i	Oct 90
6	M'bishi Galant 1.8GLSi	Mar 94
6	Nissan Primera 1.6 LS	Oct 91
6	Vauxhall Cavalier 1.6 L	Oct 87
6	Nissan Bluebird 2.0 GSX	Nov 88
6	Rover 620i	Mar 94
6	Ford Sierra 1.6 L Sapph.	Oct 87
6	Honda Accord 2.0i LS	Mar 94
6	Rover Montego 2.0 D est	Nov 89
6	Peugeot 405 1.9 GLx4	Apr 90
5	M'bishi Galant 1.8 GLS	Oct 91
5	Nissan Bluebird 1.6 LX	Oct 87
5	Peugeot 405 1.6 GLi a	Jan 93
5	Peugeot 405 GRD Estate	Nov 89
5	Ford Sierra 2.0 GL	Nov 88
5	Mazda 626 2.0i GLX	Mar 93
5	Toyota Carina 1.6 GL	Nov 88
5	Lancia Dedra 1.8 i.e.	Jun 91
5	Toyota Camry 2.0 GLi	Oct 86
5	Honda Accord EX	Oct 86
5	Subaru 1.8 GL 4wd	Apr 90
5	Mazda 626 2.0 GLX est	Nov 89
5	Renault 21 2.0 GTX	Nov 88
5	Renault 21 GTD Savanna	Nov 89
5	Peugeot 405 1.9 GR	Nov 88
5	Subaru Legacy 1.8 GL	Oct 91
5	Renault 21 1.7 GTS	Oct 87
5	Mazda 626 2.0 GLX	Oct 86
5	Fiat Tempra 1.6 SX	Oct 91
5	Nissan Bluebird 2.0 GL e	Oct 86
5	Mazda 626 2.0 GLX	Nov 88
5	Rover Montego 2.0 HL e	Oct 86
4	Citroën BX GTi	Sep 91
4	Citroën BX 19 TRS est.	Oct 86
4	Citroën 14 BX	Apr 87

EXECUTIVE CARS

11	Volvo 850 2.0 GLT	Jan 94
11	Saab 900s 2.0i	Aug 94
10	Mercedes C-180 Classic	Aug 94
9	Volvo 940 2.0 GL auto	Jan 93
9	Volvo 940 GL	Jun 92
9	Audi 100 2.0E	Mar 92
8	BMW 520i	Oct 90
8	Saab 9000i	Nov 87
8	Vauxhall Carlton 2.3 LD	Nov 89
8	Vauxhall Carlton 2.0i GLa	Jan 93

7	Rover 820i	Jun 92
7	Vauxhall Carlton 2.0i CD	Nov 87
7	Volvo 740 GLE	Feb 86
7	Audi 100 2.0E	Jan 90
7	Volvo 240 GLE auto	Apr 86
7	Volvo 240 GL Estate	Nov 89
7	Saab 900	Nov 88
7	Ford Granada 2.0 LX a sal	Jan 93
7	Toyota Camry 2.2i 16v	Jan 94
6	Peugeot 605 SLi	Mar 92
6	Citroën XM 2.0i	Oct 90
6	Rover 820e 16v Fastback	Oct 90
6	Austin Rover 820Si	Nov 87
6	Renault 25 2.2 GTX	Feb 86
6	Renault Safrane 2.0 RT	Jan 94
6	Ford Granada 2.0i GL	Oct 90
5	Hyundai Sonata 2.0i GLS	Oct 90
5	Ford Granada 2.0i Ghia	Feb 86

APPENDIX 4

FUEL ECONOMY FIGURES

Most new cars sold in the UK have to undergo a series of standard tests to determine their fuel consumption. The figures are published by the Department of Transport in a booklet 'New Car Fuel Consumption', which can be purchased from Her Majesty's Stationery Office bookshops for a small fee.

The tests are carried out by the car manufacturers themselves and result in three figures which have to be displayed on new cars in the showroom. It is also common to find these figures quoted in advertisements and they will always be found in the manufacturers' brochures.

Urban test cycle

This is designed to simulate town driving and thus give an indication of the fuel consumption you would get in towns. It is carried out in a laboratory where the equipment simulates the loads and patterns of urban driving. The maximum speed reached is 31 mph. Controversially, the cars are always tested with a warm engine, so the fuel consumption from cold starts is not included.

56 mph constant speed test

This is the figure you are still most likely to see being bandied around in advertising. It is intended to represent open-road driving, but produces in the majority of cars vastly optimistic figures which you are never likely to achieve in real life.

75 mph constant speed test

Though our national speed limit is 70 mph, this test is said to exist to show the worsening of fuel consumption at higher speeds. It also ties in well with tests done on the Continent. In reality, it is a fair method of comparing the fuel consumption of cars on motorway trips.

WHAT DO THESE FIGURES MEAN TO YOU?

Relating these figures to what you might really achieve with a new car is difficult but far from impossible. You have a number of options, listed below.

Your existing car

Look up the figures for your existing car, and see how these relate to the real-life fuel consumption figures you get for your car. If you can see some similarity between the statutory figures and what you achieve – say you typically get 10 per cent worse than the published figure – then you might read this 10 per cent reduction across to the published data for other cars you are considering.

A composite figure

Most drivers, however, only have a good idea of the overall fuel consumption their existing car achieves. You might see if this figure is close to any of the three published ones, or compare it with a commonly used composite mpg:

composite mpg =
(0.5 x urban) + (0.25 x 56mph) + (0.25 x 75mph)

Once more, see how much this composite figure compares with what you really achieve with your car, and apply the same factor to other cars you are considering.

WHICH? MEMBERS' FUEL CONSUMPTION

Each year *Which?* surveys members on the reliability of their cars for its annual *Guide to New and Used Cars*. Included in the survey is a question on the overall fuel consumption members achieve; the 1994 survey results, based on 33,000 cars, are given below. Where a car was too new for members' information, the mpg achieved in the 7,000-mile *Which?* test is given in *italics*.

Superminis and small cars

	Engine	MPG
Citroën AX	1.1	43
	1.1i	*40*
	1.4	38
Daihatsu Mira	850	46
Daihatsu Charade (May '93 onwards)	1.3	*37*
Fiat Cinquecento	0.9	*43*
Fiat Panda	750	45
	1000	41
Fiat Uno	1.1	*45*
	1.4 turbo	*31*
	auto	*38*
	1.7 diesel	*44*
Ford Fiesta	1.0	38
(pre-April '89)	1.1	38
	auto	*39*
	diesel	*50*
Ford Fiesta	1.1	42
(April '89 onwards)	1.1i	41
	XR2i	*33*
	1.3i auto	*37*
Mitsubishi Colt	1.6	34
Nissan Micra	1.0	42
(pre-Jan '93)	1.0 auto	36
	1.2	42
Nissan Micra (Jan '93 onwards)	1.0	*40*
Peugeot 106	1.1	41

Peugeot 205	1.4	38
	1.6 auto	*32*
	diesel	52
	1.6 GTi	31
Renault 5	1.1	42
	1.2	*35*
	1.4 auto	33
Renault Clio	1.2	40
	1.4	40
	1.4 auto	36
Rover Mini	1.0	42
Rover Metro	1.0	38
(pre-May '90)	1.3	37
	1.3 auto	34
Rover Metro	1.1	39
(May '90 onwards)	1.4 auto	*36*
	1.4 GTi	*37*
Seat Ibiza	1.3	*32*
(Oct '93 onwards)		
Subaru Vivio	650	45
Suzuki Swift	1.3	*43*
	1.3 GTi	*41*
Toyota Starlet	1.0	*40*
(April '90 onwards)	1.3	*40*
Vauxhall Nova	1.0	39
	1.2	39
	1.3	37
Vauxhall Corsa	1.2 E Drive	*44*
VW Polo	1.3 CL	39
	1.3 CFE	38

Small family cars

Citroën ZX	1.4	37
	1.6 auto	*30*
Fiat Tipo/Tempra	1.4	34
	1.6	35
	1.7 diesel	*43*

Ford Escort/Orion (pre-Sept '90)	1.4	35
	16	33
	1.6 diesel	*46*
Ford Escort/Orion (Sept '90 onwards)	1.4	33
	1.6	33
	1.8	33
	1.8 diesel	48
Honda Civic (Oct '87–Dec '91)	1.3	39
	1.4	37
Honda Civic (Dec '91 onwards)	1.5	*37*
Honda Concerto	1.6	32
Hyundai Lantra	1.6	31
Lada Riva	1.2	33
	1.3	33
	1.5	32
Lada Samara	1.3	*33*
Mazda 323 (Oct '89 onwards)	1.6	35
Nissan Sunny (pre-March '91)	1.3	37
	1.4	37
	1.6	36
Nissan Sunny (March '91 onwards)	1.4	37
	1.6	*34*
	1.6 auto	*32*
Peugeot 306	1.6	*32*
Peugeot 309	1.3	36
	1.6	33
	diesel	50
Proton MPi	1.5	37
Renault 19	1.4	38
	1.7	33
	diesel	*44*
Rover Maestro	1.3	35
	1.6	35
	1.6 auto	30
	2.0	32

Rover 200	1.3	38
(pre-Oct '89)	1.6	33
	1.6 EFi	35
Rover 200	1.4	36
(Oct '89 onwards)	1.6	35
	1.6 auto	32
	diesel	*44*
Skoda Favorit	1.3	38
Subaru Impreza	1.8	*28*
Toyota Corolla	1.3	38
(Sept '87–Aug '92)	1.6	34
	1.6 4WD	*28*
Toyota Corolla	1.3	39
(Sept '92 onwards)		
Vauxhall Astra/Belmont	1.3	35
(Oct '84–Oct '91)	1.4	37
	1.6	36
	1.6 diesel	49
Vauxhall Astra	1.4i	39
(Oct '91 onwards)	1.6i	36
VW Golf	1.3	35
(March '84–March '92)	1.6	34
	GTi	35
	diesel	50
VW Golf/Vento	1.4	*38*
(March '92 onwards)	1.8 CL	34
	2.0 GL	*32*
Volvo 340	1.4	34
	1.4 auto	30
	1.7	33
	2.0	30
Large family cars		
Audi 80	1.8	34
(Oct '86–Dec '91)		
Audi 80	2.0	32
(Dec '91 onwards)		

BMW 3 Series	1.6	32
(old shape)	2.0	*27*
	2.5	*27*
BMW 3 Series	1.6	*32*
(new shape)	1.6 auto	*29*
	1.8	32
Citroën BX	1.4	36
	1.6	32
	1.9 TRS	32
	1.9 diesel	47
Citroën Xantia	1.8	*30*
Ford Sierra/Sapphire	1.6	31
	2.0	32
	2.0 auto	*27*
	2.3 diesel	*38*
Ford Mondeo	1.8	32
Honda Accord	2.0	30
(Oct '89–May '94)		
Honda Accord	2.0	*31*
(May '93 onwards)		
Lancia Dedra	1.8	*29*
Mazda 626	2.0	29
(Oct '87–March '92)		
Mazda 626	2.0	*32*
(March '92 onwards)		
Mitsubishi Galant	1.8	*30*
(pre-March '93)		
Mitsubishi Galant	1.8	*34*
(March '93 onwards)		
Nissan Bluebird	1.6	33
	1.8	32
	2.0	31
Nissan Primera	1.6	35
	2.0	31
Peugeot 405	1.6 auto	*30*
	1.9	33
	diesel	48
	4x4	*29*

Renault 21	1.7	33
	2.0	31
	2.1 diesel	*39*
Rover Montego	1.6	33
	1.6 auto	29
	2.0	32
	Turbo diesel	49
Rover 600	2.0	*30*
Seat Toledo	1.8	*32*
Subaru Legacy (pre-March '94)	1.8	*28*
Toyota Carina (April '88–May '92)	1.6	36
	1.6 auto	33
	2.0	33
Toyota Carina E (May '92 onwards)	2.0	34
Vauxhall Cavalier (pre-Oct '88)	1.3	33
	1.6	33
	1.8 auto	31
Vauxhall Cavalier (Oct '88 onwards)	1.6	36
	1.8	35
	2.0	34
VW Passat (May '88 onwards)	1.6 Turbo diesel	*43*
	1.8	34
	2.0	35
Volvo 440/460	1.7	32

Executive cars

Audi 100 (pre-May '91)	2.0	*28*
	2.1	*30*
Audi 100 (May '91 onwards)	2.0	*30*
BMW 5 Series (Mar '88 onwards)	2.0	26
	2.5 auto	24
Citroën XM	2.0	29
Ford Granada	2.0i	31
	2.0i auto	29
	2.9i auto	24

Mercedes-Benz 190	2.0	30
	2.0 diesel	*43*
Peugeot 605	2.0	*28*
Renault 25	2.0	31
	2.2	32
	2.2 auto	*25*
Renault Safrane	2.0	*27*
Rover 800	2.0e	31
	2.0i	32
	2.7 auto	25
Saab 900 (pre-Nov '93)	2.0	28
	2.3	29
	Turbo	28
Saab 9000/CD	2.0	30
	2.0 auto	27
Toyota Camry (Oct '91 onwards)	2.2	*29*
Vauxhall Carlton	2.0	31
	2.0 auto	29
	2.3 diesel	*36*
Volvo 240	2.0	28
	2.3	27
	2.3 auto	24
Volvo 700	2.0	29
	2.3	28
	2.3 auto	26
Volvo 850	2.0	28
Volvo 900	2.0	*27*
	2.0 auto	*25*

APPENDIX 5

CUSTOMER CARE CONTACTS

Every car manufacturer and importer runs a customer care department. These are useful on two counts – they can provide you with up-to-date information and brochures on the latest models, and they are your point of contact if things go really wrong in your relationship with your dealer. Remember, though, that legally any problems with a car should be sorted out with the supplying dealer – the customer care department of the manufacturer and importer is there to help things along, rather than as the primary port of call.

Alfa Romeo GB
266 Batch Road
Slough
Berkshire
SL1 4HL
(0753) 511431

BMW (GB) Ltd
Ellesfield Avenue
Bracknell
Berkshire
RG12 7TA
(0344) 426565

Citroën UK Ltd
221 Bath Road
Slough
Berkshire
SL1 4BA
(0753) 822100

Daihatsu (UK) Ltd
Poulton Close
Dover
Kent
CT17 0HP
(0304) 213030

Fiat Auto (UK) Ltd
266 Batch Road
Slough
Berkshire
SL1 4HL
(0753) 511431

Ford Motor Co. Ltd
Ford Central Office
Eagle Way
Brentwood
Essex CM13 3BW
(0800) 231231

Honda UK
Power Road
Chiswick
London W4 5YT
081-747 1400

Hyundai (UK) Ltd
Ryder Street
West Bromwich
Birmingham B70 0JE
021-522 2882

Lada Cars
3120 Park Square
Birmingham Business Park
Birmingham B37 7YN
021-717 9000

Mazda Cars (UK)
77 Mount Ephraim
Tunbridge Wells
Kent TN4 8BS
(0892) 511877

Mercedes-Benz (UK) Ltd
Tongwell
Milton Keynes
Buckinghamshire MK15 8BA
(0908) 245000

Mitsubishi Motors
The Colt Car Company Limited
Watermoor
Cirencester
Gloucestershire GL7 1LF
(0285) 655777

Nissan Motor (GB)
The Rivers Office Park
Denham Way
Maple Cross
Rickmansworth
Hertfordshire WD3 2YS
(0923) 899999

Peugeot Motor Company
Aldermoor House
Aldermoor Lane
Coventry CV3 1LT
(0203) 884000

Proton Cars (UK) Ltd
Proton House
Royal Portbury Dock
Bristol
Avon BS20 0NH
(0275) 375475

Renault UK Ltd
Rivermead Industrial Estate
Westlea
Swindon
Wiltshire SN5 7YA
(0793) 513888

Rover Cars
PO Box 47
Cowley Body Plant
Oxford OX4 5NL
(0800) 620820

Saab
Saab House
Globe Park
Marlow
Buckinghamshire SL1 1LY
(0628) 895603

Seat (UK) Ltd
Seat House
Gatwick Road
Crawley
West Sussex RH10 2AX
(0293) 514141

Skoda UK Ltd
Garamond Drive
Great Monks Street
Wymbush
Milton Keynes
Buckinghamshire
MK8 8NZ
(0908) 264000

Subaru (UK) Ltd
Ryder Street
West Bromwich
Birmingham B70 0JE
021-522 2000

Suzuki GB Cars Ltd
46–62 Gatwick Road
Crawley
West Sussex RH10 2XF

Toyota (GB) Ltd
The Quadrangle
Redhill
Surrey RH1 1PX
(0737) 768585

Vauxhall Motors
Osbourne Road
Luton
Bedfordshire
LU1 3YT
(0582) 427200

Volkswagen Audi
VAG (UK) Ltd
Yeoman's Drive
Blakelands
Milton Keynes
Buckinghamshire
MK14 5AN
(0908) 601800

Volvo Cars UK Ltd
Globe Park
Marlow
Buckinghamshire
SL7 1YQ
(0628) 477977

APPENDIX 6

New Car Guarantees

Make of car	General guarantee	Anti-perforation rust warranty	Paintwork warranty	Breakdown recovery
Alfa Romeo	1 year	8 years	3 years	1 year
Audi	1 year	10 years	3 years	up to 6 years
BMW	3 years/60,000 miles[1]	6 years	3 years	3 years/60,000 miles[1]
Citroën	1 year	6 years	1 year	1 year
Daihatsu	3 years	6 years	3 years	1 year
Fiat	1 year	8 years	3 years	1 year
Ford	1 year	6 years	1 year	1 year
Honda	2 years	6 years	3 years	2 years
Hyundai	3 years	6 years	3 years	3 years
Lada	2 years/50,000 miles	6 years	1 year	1 year
Mazda	3 years/60,000 miles	6 years	6 years	3 years
Mazda Xedos	3 years/60,000 miles	8 years	6 years	3 years
Mercedes-Benz	1 year	1 year	1 year	4 years
Mitsubishi	3 years	6 years	3 years	3 years
Nissan	3 years/60,000 miles	6 years	3 years	1 year
Peugeot	1 year	6 years	1 year	1 year
Proton Cars	2 years/50,000 miles	6 years	2 years	2 years

Renault	1 year	8 years	1 year	1 year
Rover	1 year	6 years	3 years	1 year
Saab	1 or 3 years/60,000 miles[2]	6 years	6 years	1 year
Seat	1 year	6 years	1 year	1 year
Skoda	2 years	6 years	2 years	2 years
Subaru	3 years/60,000 miles	6 years	1 year	3 years
Suzuki	3 years/60,000 miles	6 years	3 years	1 year
Toyota	3 years/60,000 miles	6 years	3 years	1 year
Vauxhall	1 year	6 years	1 year	1 year
Volkswagen	1 year	6 years	3 years	up to 6 years
Volvo	3 years/60,000 miles	8 years	3 years	1 year

Note: All warranties are for an unlimited mileage, unless otherwise noted.

1 BMW warranty comprises one year's manufacturer warranties, plus an extra two years organised by BMW dealers if you have your car serviced at a franchised dealer.

2 Second and third years of Saab warranty apply only to major mechanical components and this is restricted to 60,000 miles.

INDEX